Schwerpunktthema

Abitur Englisch

Short Stories from Australia

Cornelsen

Short Stories from Australia

Herausgegeben von

Marcus Hemjeoltmanns

Verlagsredaktion

Neil Porter

Layout und technische Umsetzung

Buchgestaltung+, Berlin

Umschlaggestaltung

Hawemann & Mosch

www.cornelsen.de

1. Auflage, 2. Druck 2010

Alle Drucke dieser Auflage sind inhaltlich unverändert und können im Unterricht nebeneinander verwendet werden.

Druck: CS-Druck CornelsenStürtz, Berlin

ISBN 978-3-06-032513-9

Inhalt gedruckt auf säurefreiem Papier aus nachhaltiger Forstwirtschaft.

Contents

Abbreviations and symbols

adj	adjective
abbr	abbreviation
AustrEng	Australian English
cf.	confer, see
derog	derogatory
ed.	editor
e.g.	(Latin) exempli gratia = for example
esp.	especially
etc.	(Latin) et cetera = and so on
ff.	and the following lines/pages
fml	formal
i.e.	(Latin) id est = that is
infml	informal
jdm.	jemandem
jdn.	jemanden
l., ll.	line, lines
n	noun
p., pp.	page, pages
pl	plural
sb.	somebody
sl	slang
sth.	something
usu.	usually
v	verb
vulg	vulgar

Introduction

Australian literature developed slowly over the 19th century. The settlers' main preoccupation was to make a living out of the land rather than to write literature in their new country. The first writings from Australia were reports of life in Australia, emphasizing the alien in the new Continent: the different landscape and plants, the experience with Aborigines. The discovery of gold in 1851 brought many more settlers to the country and a lot more prosperity, resulting in the publication of more newspapers and magazines, some of which started to publish poems and stories. One particular weekly, *The Bulletin*, was responsible for encouraging literature from the bush, usually stories about men in the outback (the first three stories in this collection were all first published in *The Bulletin*). A national literature started to develop in which characters like convicts, bushmen, etc. were seen as being important figures in Australian life.

Since the arrival of Europeans, Australia has been a country dominated by conflict and tension between groups of people: between whites and aborigines, convicts and freemen, city dwellers and bushmen, Anglos and Mediterraneans, Europeans and Asians. Through these tensions a particular national Australian identity has been formed and will continue to be formed. Each of the five stories here deals with a different aspect of Australia identity.

While reading these stories, consider the following questions:

- What sort of characters do you encounter?
- What makes these characters 'Australian'?
- What conflicts and tensions emerge between the individuals or groups at the centre of the stories?
- What do the conflicts reveal about Australian identity?
- What role does nature play in the story and what impact does it have on the lives of the characters?

Accompanying each story is information about the author, an Infobox with information about an aspect dealt with in the story, tasks and an additional text which is of relevance to the story.

PRICE WARUNG **How Muster-Master Stoneman Earned His Breakfast**

William Astley (1855–1911) was a journalist and author who wrote under the pseudonym 'Price Warung'. He was born in Liverpool and emigrated with his family to Melbourne in 1859. Astley worked for several Australian newspapers and magazines. In the early 1890s he won recognition as a short-story writer. His stories give an insight into early Australian history and always rely on carefully investigated data or personal testimony. The first collection of these, *Tales of the Convict System*, from which this story is taken, appeared in 1892; this was followed by *Tales of the Early Days* (1894), *Tales of the Old Regime* (1897), *Tales of the Isle of Death* (1898) and *Half-Crown Bob and Tales of the Riverine* (1898). His stories dealing with the convict system criticize the cruel and inhumane rule of the British administrators. Throughout his life he remained a fierce opponent of British imperialism. In his final years he suffered from mental illness and died in Rookwood Benevolent Asylum in Sydney.

The short story 'How Muster-Master Stoneman Earned His Breakfast' is an example of Price Warung's writing about the convict system. From 1787 to 1868 British criminals were shipped to Australian penal colonies run by British authorities, where they were treated harshly. The story was published in 1890.

I.

An unpretentious building of rough-hewn stone standing in the middle of a small, stockaded enclosure. A doorway in the wall of the building facing the entrance-gate to the yard. To the left of the doorway, a glazed window of the ordinary size. To its right a paneless aperture, so low and narrow that were the four upright and two transverse bars which grate it doubled in thickness no interstice would be left for the admission of light or air to the interior. Behind the bars – a face.

Sixteen hours hence that face will look its last upon the world which has stricken it countless cruel blows. In a corner of the enclosure the executioner's hand is even now busy stitching into a shapeless cap, a square of grey serge. Tomorrow the same hand will use the cap to hood the face, as one of the few simple preliminaries to swinging the carcase to which the face is attached from the rude platform now in course of erection against the stockade fence and barely 20 yards in front of the stone building.

• *muster-master* ['mʌstə] official who is in charge of troops or (here) convicts
1 *unpretentious* [ˌʌnprɪ'tenʃəs] modest, simple
1 *rough-hewn stone* stone that has a rough surface
2 *stockaded* von Palisaden (= Holzpfählen) umgeben
2 *enclosure* area that is sealed off by a barrier
4 *glazed window* window that contains a sheet of glass
5 *paneless* without a sheet of glass
5 *aperture* opening
5 *were* if ... were
6 *transverse* horizontal
6 *grate sth.* (of bars) cover sth.
7 *interstice* [ɪn'tɜ:stɪs] small space
9 *sixteen hours hence* in sixteen hours
12 *serge* type of strong cloth
13 *hood sb.* put a hood (= Kapuze) over the head of sb.
14 *preliminary* action done in preparation for sth.
14 *carcase* (usu. *carcass*) dead body usu. of an animal
15 *rude* roughly made

The building is the goal – locally known as the 'cage' – of Oatlands, a small township in the midlands of Van Dieman's Land, which has gradually grown up round a convict 'muster-station', established by Governor Davey. The time is five o'clock on a September evening, 55 years ago. At nine o'clock on the following morning, Convict Glancy, No. 17,927, transportee *ex* ship Pestonjee Bomanjee (second trip), originally under sentence for seven years for the theft of a silk handkerchief from a London 'swell', will suffer the extreme penalty of the law for having, in an intemperate moment, objected to the mild discipline with which a genial and loving motherland had sought to correct his criminal tendencies. In other words, Convict Glancy, metaphorically goaded by the wordy insults and literally by the bayonet-tip of one of his motherland's reformatory agents – to wit, Road-gang Overseer James Jones – had scattered J.J.'s brains over a good six square yards of metalled roadway. The deed has been rapturously applauded by Glancy's fellow-gangers, all of whom had the inclination, but lacked the courage, to wield the crowbar that has been the means of erasing this particular tyrant's name from the pay-sheets of His Britannic Majesty's Colonial Penal Establishment. Nevertheless and notwithstanding such tribute of appreciation, H.B.M.'s Colonial representatives, police, judicial and gubernatorial, have thought it rather one to be censured and have, accordingly, left Convict Glancy for execution.

This decision of the duly-constituted authorities Convict Glancy has somewhat irrelevantly (as it will seem to us at this enlightened day) acknowledged by a fervent 'Thank God!' – an ejaculation rendered the more remarkable by the fact that never before in his convict history had he linked the name of the Deity with any expression of gratitude for the many blessings enjoyed by him in that state of penal servitude to which it had pleased the same Deity to call him. On the contrary, he had constantly indulged in maledictions on his fate and on his Maker. He had resolutely cursed the benignant forces with which the System and the King's Regulations had surrounded him, and he had failed to reverence as he ought the triangles, the gang-chains, the prodding bayonet, and the other things which would have conduced to his reformation had he but manifested a more humble and obedient spirit. No wonder, therefore, as Chaplain Ford said, that it has come about that he has qualified for the capital doom.

Upon this doom, in so far as it could be represented by the gallows, Convict Glancy was now gazing with an unflinching eye. On this September evening he stands at his

18 *gaol* [dʒeɪl] (BE spelling) jail
19 *Van Dieman's Land* former name of Tasmania
20 *convict muster-station* (here) place where convicts are kept
21 *Governor Davey* governor of Van Dieman's Land (1813–1816)
24 *transportee* convict that has been taken from one place to another
24 *ex* (Latin) from
25 *sentence* punishment given by a court
26 *swell* (infml) fashionable or stylish wealthy person
27 *intemperate* showing a lack of self-control
28 *genial* ['dʒiːniəl] kind and friendly
31 *goad sb.* annoy sb. in order to provoke a reaction
32 *reformatory agent* (here) person who helps prisoners become better people
32 *to wit* that is to say
32 *road-gang* group of prisoners who build roads
33 *overseer* person in charge of others
33 *scatter sth.* throw sth. in different directions
34 *metalled* covered with crushed rock (= Schotter)
35 *rapturous* showing great pleasure
35 *fellow-gangers* (here) the other members of the road-gang
37 *crowbar* Brechstange
41 *gubernatorial* relating to a governor
42 *censure sth.* criticize sth.
44 *duly-constituted* ordnungsgemäß gebildet
46 *enlightened* that is not based on old-fashioned attitudes
46 *fervent* intensely passionate
47 *ejaculation* Ausruf
47 *render sth.* make sth.
49 *the Deity* God
52 *indulge in sth.* [ɪn'dʌldʒ] sich zu etwas hinreißen lassen
52 *malediction* curse
53 *maker* Schöpfer
53 *benignant* kind and merciful
55 *reverence sth.* etwas mit Ehrfurcht betrachten
56 *triangle* wooden triangle to which convicts were tied for whipping
56 *gang-chain* chain used to tie a group of convicts together
56 *prod sb.* push sb. with a pointed object
58 *had he but* ... if he had only ...
58 *manifest sth.* show sth., reveal sth.
58 *humble* showing you do not think you are important
59 *chaplain* ['tʃæplɪn] Kaplan
60 *capital doom* death sentence
63 *gallows* (pl) Galgen
63 *unflinching* that did not move

cell-window looking on half-a-dozen brown-clothed figures handling saw, and square, and hammer, as they fix in the earth two sturdy uprights, and to those a projecting cross-beam; as they bind the two with a solid tie-piece of knotless hardwood; as they build a narrow platform of planks around the gallows-tree; as they fasten a rope to the notched end of the cross beam; and as they slope to the edge of the planks,

66 *square* Winkelmaß
67 *upright* vertical post
67 *cross-beam* Querbalken
68 *tie-piece* piece of wood that connects to things
68 *knotless* ohne Astknoten
70 *notched* eingekerbt

Infobox | Convicts in Australia

The Industrial Revolution had seen a dramatic increase in population and in urban poverty in Britain. Prisons were generally overcrowded and the conditions were appalling. Transportation was a common punishment handed out for both major and petty crimes in Britain from the 17th century. Around 60,000 convicts had been transported to the British colonies in North America, but after American independence the British government was forced to look else-where. After Captain Cook's famous voyage to the South Pacific in which he visited and claimed Australia in the name of the British Empire (1770), the British, for the first time, became aware of the existence of the continent of Australia. In order to establish a foothold on the other side of the globe, it was decided to establish a penal colony in Australia. The penal system required the convicts to work on government projects such as road construction, building works and mining, or to be assigned to free individuals as unpaid labour. Women were expected to work as domestic servants and farm labourers. In 1788 what is referred to as 'the First Fleet' of 11 ships arrived in Port Jackson (now Sydney) with about 1500 people, including 778 convicts (192 women and 586 men), to establish the first European colony in Australia. Until transportation was discontinued in 1868 approximately 160,000 convicts had been sent to Australia. The Pestonjee Bomanjee (cf. l. 24) was one of numerous ships that travelled back and forth between England and Australia. As free settlers started arriving in large numbers in the 1820s, it was no longer considered necessary to use convicts to settle the land.

THE CONVICT SHIP.

ten feet from the ground, a rude ladder. All the drowsy afternoon he had watched the working party, though Chaplain Ford had stood by his side droning of the grace which had been withheld from him in life, but might still be his in death. He had felt interested, had Convict Glancy, in these preparations for the event in which he was to act such a prominent part on the morrow. He had even laughed at the grim humour of one of the brown-garbed workers who, when the warder's eye was off him, had gone through the pantomime of noosing the rope-end round his own neck – a little joke which contributed much to the (necessarily noiseless) delight of the rest of the gang.

Altogether, Convict Glancy reflected as dusk fell, and the working party gathered up their tools, and the setting sun tipped the bayonets of the guard with a diamond iridescence, that he had spent many a duller afternoon. If the Chaplain had only held his tongue, the time would have passed with real pleasantness. He said as much to the good man as the latter remarked to the warder on duty in the cell that he would look in again after supper.

'You may save yourself the trouble, sir,' quoth, respectfully enough, Convict Glancy. 'You have spoilt my last afternoon. Don't spoil my last night!'

Chaplain Ford winced at the words. He was still comparatively new to the work of spiritually superintending a hundred or so monsters who looked upon the orthodox hell as a place where residence would be pleasantly recreative after Port Arthur Settlement and Norfolk Island; and the time lay still in the future when, being completely embruted, he would come to regard it as a very curious circumstance indeed that Christ had omitted eulogistic reference to the System from the Sermon on the Mount. Consequently he winced and sighed, not so much – to do him justice – at the utter depravity of Convict Glancy as at his own inability to reach the reprobate's heart. But he took the hint; he mournfully said he would not return that evening, but would be with the prisoner by half-past 5 o'clock in the morning.

II.

When Chaplain Ford entered the enclosure immediately before the hour he had named, he at once understood, from the excitement manifested by a group assembled in front of the 'cage', that something was amiss. Voices were uttering fearful words, impetuously, almost shriekingly, and hands swung lanterns – the grey dawn had not yet driven the darkness from the stockade – and brandished muskets furiously.

72 *drowsy* making you feel tired (due to heat, etc.)
74 *drone* speak slowly and in a boring way
74 *grace* Gottes Gnade
75 *withhold sth. from sb.* not give sb. sth.
78 *the morrow* the following day
79 *brown-garbed* dressed in brown clothes
80 *warder* prison guard
81 *noose sth.* make a noose (= Schlinge) out of sth.
84 *dusk* Abenddämmerung
86 *iridescence* [ˌɪrɪ'desəns] Schillern
87 *dull* boring
92 *quoth* (old use) said
95 *wince* zusammenzucken
96 *superintend sb./sth.* be in charge of sb./sth. and make sure that everything is alright
97 *orthodox hell* hell as it is traditionally imagined
98 *residence* act of living somewhere
98 *recreative* enjoyable
99 *Port Arthur Settlement, Norfolk Island* places that served as prisons
100 *embruted* having become a brutal uncaring person
102 *omit sth.* leave sth. out, exclude sth.
102 *eulogistic* [ju:lə'dʒɪstɪk] praising sb./sth. highly
103 *Sermon on the Mount* Bergpredigt
105 *utter* complete, absolute
105 *depravity* Verdorbenheit
106 *reprobate* person who is totally immoral
112 *amiss* wrong
112 *utter sth.* say sth.
113 *impetuous* done quickly without thinking
114 *lantern* lamp
115 *brandish sth.* etwas wedeln, mit etwas herumfuchteln
115 *musket* old type of gun

A very brief space of time served to inform the reverend functionary what had gone wrong.

Convict Glancy had made his escape, having previously murdered, with the victim's own bayonet, the warder who had been told-off to watch him during the night. This latter circumstance was, of course, unfortunate, but alone it would not have created the excitement, for the murder of prison-officials was a common enough occurrence. It was the other thing that galled the gesticulating and blaspheming group. That a prisoner, fettered with ten-pound irons, should have broken out of gaol on the very eve of his execution – why, it was calculated to shake the confidence of the Comptroller-General himself in the infallibility and perfect righteousness of the System. And, popular and authoritative belief in the System once shattered, where would they be?

The murdered man had gone on duty at 10 o'clock, and very shortly afterwards he must have met with his fate. How Glancy had obtained possession of the bayonet could only be conjectured. As was the custom during the day or two preceding a convict's execution, he had been left unmanacled, and ironed with double leg-chains only. Thus his hands were free to perpetrate the deed once he grasped the weapon. Glancy, on his escape, had taken the instrument with him, but there was no doubt that he had inflicted death with it, the wound in the dead man's breast being obviously caused by the regulation bayonet. Possibly the sentinel had nodded, and then a violent wrench of the prisoner's wrist and a sudden stab had extended his momentary slumber into an eternal sleep. The bayonet had also been used by Glancy to prise up a flooring-flag, and to scoop out an aperture under the wall, the basestones of which, following the slipshod architecture of the time, rested on the surface and were not sunk into the ground.

The work of excavation must have taken the convict several hours, and must have been conducted as noiselessly as the manner of committing the crime itself. A solitary warder occupied the outer guard-room, but he asserted that he had heard no sound except the exchange of whistle-signals between the dormitory guard at the convict-barracks (a quarter-of-mile away at the rear of the gaol-stockade) and the military patrol. The night routine of the 'cage' did not insist upon the whistle-signal between the men on duty, but they passed a simple 'All's well' every hour. And this the guardroom-warder maintained he had done with the officer inside the condemned cell, the response being given in a low tone, from consideration, so the former thought, for the sleeping convict so soon to die. Of course, if this man was to be be-

116 *reverend functionary* church official
120 *tell sb. off* (here) give sb. a task
124 *gall sb.* make sb. very annoyed
124 *blaspheme* [blæs'fiːm] use swear words
125 *fetter sb.* put chains on sb.'s feet
126 *eve* day before something
127 *Comptroller-General* (formerly) person in charge of convicts in a state or territory
128 *infallability* Unfehlbarkeit
128 *righteousness* state of being morally right
130 *shatter sth.* destroy sth.
134 *conjecture sth.* form an opinion about sth. based on little information
134 *preceding* before
135 *unmanacled* [ʌn'mænəkəld] not wearing hand chains
137 *perpetrate sth.* carry out sth. (esp. an illegal action)
137 *deed* Tat
141 *regulation* as used by the army
141 *sentinel* soldier on guard
141 *nod* (here) fall asleep
142 *wrench* violent twist or pull
143 *stab* Stoß
143 *slumber* sleep
144 *prise sth.* open sth. by force
145 *flag* Steinplatte, Fliese
145 *scoop out* (here) dig with your hands
146 *slipshod* lacking in care, thought or organization
149 *excavation* Ausgrabung
150 *conduct sth.* carry sth. out
152 *assert sth.* state sth. confidently
154 *dormitory* sleeping room for several people
155 *at the rear of sth.* at the back of sth.
160 *condemned cell* cell for a prisoner who is condemned to death
161 *former* the first-mentioned of two people

A road-gang accompanied by British soldiers

lieved, Glancy must have uttered the words. It was not the first time the signal which should have been given by a prison officer had been made by his convict murderer.

The murderer was discovered on the arrival of the relief watch at five o'clock. The last 'All's well' was exchanged at four. Consequently the escapee had less than an hour's start. The scaling of the stockade would not be difficult even for a man in irons, and once in the bush an experienced hand would soon find a method of fracturing the links.

It must be admitted that this contumacious proceeding of Convict Glancy was most vexatious. Under-Sheriff Ropewell, now soundly reposing at the township inn, would be forthcoming at 9 o'clock with his Excellency's warrant in his hand to demand from Muster-Master Stoneman the body of one James Glancy, and Muster-Master Stoneman would have to apologise for his inability to produce the said body. The difficulty was quite unprecedented, and Stoneman, as he stood in the midst of his minions, groaned audibly at the prospect of having to do the thing most abhorrent to the official mind – establish a precedent.

'Such a thing was never heard!' he cried. 'A man to bolt just when he was to be turned off? And the d––d hypocrite tried to make his Honor and all of us think that he was only too happy to be scragged. It's too d––d bad!'

It certainly did seem peculiar that Glancy, who had apparently much rejoiced at the contemplation of his early decease, should give leg-bail just when he was to realise his wishes. He had told the judge that 'he was –– glad they were going to kill him right off instead of by inches,' and yet he had voluntarily thrown off the noose when it was virtually round his neck. Was it the mere contrariness of the convict nature that prompted the escape? Or, was it the innate love of life that becomes stronger as the benefits of living become fewer and fewer? Had the craving for existence and for

166 *relief watch* ablösender Wachsoldat
169 *scale sth.* climb up or over sth.
171 *fracture sth.* break sth.
172 *contumacious* [ˌkɒntju'meɪʃəs] disobedient to authority
173 *vexatious* [vek'seɪʃəs] causing annoyance
174 *soundly* very deeply
174 *repose* (here) sleep
174 *inn* pub providing food and rooms
175 *be forthcoming* appear
175 *his Excellency* (here) the governor
175 *warrant* official paper demanding sth.
179 *unprecedented* [ʌn'presɪdentɪd] never known before
180 *minion* unimportant person who is lower in rank
181 *abhorrent* causing hatred
182 *precedent* decision that is seen as a rule for similar cases in the future
183 *bolt* run away
184 *turn sb. off* (here) execute sb.
184 *d-d* damned
185 *his Honor* der Vorsitzende Richter
186 *scrag sb.* (infml) hang sb.
188 *rejoice* feel or show great joy
188 *contemplation* Betrachtung
188 *decease* death
189 *give leg-bail* (infml) escape
192 *virtually* nearly, almost
193 *contrariness* Widerspenstigkeit
194 *prompt sth.* cause sth.
194 *innate* inborn, natural
196 *craving* powerful desire

freedom surged over his despair and recklessness at the eleventh hour?

Such were the enquiries which Chaplain Ford put to himself as, horrified, he took in the particulars of No. 17,927's crowning enormities from the hubbub of the group.

'Damn it!' said the Muster-Master at last, 'we are losing time. The devil can't have gone far with those ten-pounders on him. We'll have to put the regulars on the track as well as our own men. Warder Briggs, report to Captain White at the barracks, and ...'

Muster-Master Stoneman stopped short. Through the foggy air there came the familiar sound as of a convict dragging his irons. What could it be? No prisoners had been as yet loosed from the dormitory. Whence could the noise proceed?

Clink – clank – s-sh – dr-g-g – clink – clank – dr-g-g. The sound drew nearer, and Convict Glancy turned in at the enclosure gateway – unescorted. He had severed the leg-chain at the link which connected with the basil of the left anklet, but had not taken the trouble to remove the other part of the chain. Thus, while he could take his natural pace with his left foot, he dragged the fetters behind his right leg.

A moment of hushed surprise, and then three or four men rushed towards him. The first who touched him he felled with a blow.

'Not yet,' said he, grimly. 'I give myself up, Mr Stoneman – you don't take me! I give myself up – you ain't going to get ten quid for taking me.' And then Convict Glancy laughed, and held out his hands for the handcuffs. He laughed more heartily as the subordinate hirelings of the System threw themselves upon him like hounds on their prey.

'No need to turn out the sodgers now, Muster-Master – not till nine o'clock.' Once more his hideous laugh rang through the yards. 'You had an easier job than you expected, hadn't you, Stoneman, old cove?'

Muster-Master Stoneman had been surprised into silence and into an unusual abstinence from blasphemy by the re-appearance – quite unprecedented under the circumstances! – of the doomed wretch. But the desperado's jeering tones whipped him into speech.

'Curse you!' he yelled. 'I'll teach you to laugh on the other side of your mouth presently. You'd better have kept away.' He literally foamed in his mad anger.

'Do you think I couldn't have stopped away if I'd wanted to, having got clear?' A lofty scorn rang out in the words. 'But do you think I was going to run away when I was so near

197 *surge* increase suddenly and powerfully
197 *recklessness* Leichtsinn, Rücksichtslosigkeit
197 *at the eleventh hour* at the last moment
200 *particulars* (pl) details
201 *crowning enormities* (here) acts that are impressive
201 *hubbub* chaotic noise caused by a crowd
204 *regular* normal soldier
210 *loose sb.* (old use) free sb.
210 *whence* from where
214 *sever sth.* divide sth. by cutting through it
215 *basil* Fußfessel
221 *fell sb.* knock sb. down
224 *quid* (infml) one pound sterling; ten quid was the reward paid by the government on the re-capture of an escaped prisoner.
226 *subordinate* lower in rank or position
226 *hireling* (derog) Mietling
227 *hound* dog used for hunting
228 *prey* Beute
229 *turn sb. out* call sb. out to perform a duty
229 *sodger* (infml) soldier
232 *cove* (infml) man
236 *wretch* unfortunate person
236 *desperado* bold criminal
240 *foam* schäumen
241 *stop away* remain away
242 *clear* safe, out of reach
242 *lofty* (here) arrogant
242 *scorn* Verachtung

Freedom as that?' And the wretch jerked his manacled hands in the direction of the gallows. 'You d––d fool!'

No one spoke for a full half-minute. Then: 'Why did you break gaol then?' asked the Muster-Master.

'Because I wanted to spit on Jones' grave!' was the reply.

III.

Muster-Master Stoneman was as good as his word. Death couldn't drive the smile from Glancy's face. That could only be done by one think – the lash.

When next the Muster-Master spoke it was to order the prisoner a double ration of cocoa and bread. And, 'Briggs,' he continued, 'while he is getting it, see that the triangles are rigged.'

'The triangles, sir!' exclaimed Officer Briggs and Convict Glancy together.

'I said the triangles, and I mean the triangles. No. 17,927 has broken gaol, and as Muster-Master of this station, and governor of this gaol, and as a magistrate of the territory, I can give him 750 lashes for escaping. But as he has to go through another little ceremony this morning I'll let him off with a "canary" ' – (a hundred lashes.)

'You surely cannot mean it, sir!' exclaimed Parson Ford.

'Mean it, sir! By G––, I'll show you I mean it,' replied the M.M., whose blaspheming no presence restrained save that of his official superiors. 'Give him the cocoa, Warder Tuff, give the doctor my compliments, and tell him his attendance is required here. Tell him he'd better bring his smelling-salts – they may be wanted,' he sneered in conclusion.

'You devil!' cried Glancy. The reckless grin passed away, and his face faded to the pallor of the death he was so soon to die.

As Muster-Master Stoneman turned on his heel to prepare the warrant for the flogging, he looked at his watch. It was half-past six.

At seven o'clock the first lash from the cat-o'-nine-tails fell upon Convict Glancy's back.

At 7.30 his groaning and bleeding body, which had received the full hundred of flaying stripes, lay on the pallet of the cell where he had murdered the night-guard but a few hours before.

At eight o'clock Executioner Johnson entered the cell. 'I've brought yer sumthink to 'arden yer, Glancy, ol' man. I'll rub it in, an' it'll help yer to keep up.' So tender a sympathy inspired Mr Johnson's words that anyone not knowing him

251 *lash* whip
255 *rig sth.* assemble sth.
260 *magistrate* civil officer who administers the law
265 *G––* God
266 *restrain sb.* prevent sb. from doing sth
266 *save* except
270 *sneer* smile or speak in an unpleasant manner
272 *reckless* without thought or care for a consequence of an action
273 *pallor* pale colour of the face
276 *flog sb.* beat sb. with a whip or stick
278 *cat-o'-nine-tails* whip with nine strings
281 *flay* remove the skin of a person
281 *pallet* straw mattress
285 *sumthink to 'arden yer* something to harden you
285 *ol'* old

would have thought he was the bearer of some priceless balsam. But Convict Glancy knew him; and, maddened by pain though he was, had still sensibility enough left to make a shuddering resistance to the hangman as he proceeded to rub into the gashed flesh a handful of coarse salt. 'By the Muster-Master's orders, sonny,' soothingly remarked Johnson. 'To 'arden' yer.'

At 8.45 Under-Sheriff Ropewell, who had been apprised while at breakfast of the murder and escape, appeared on the scene escorted by his javelin-men. This gentleman, too, had been greatly perplexed by Convict Glancy's proceedings. 'Really it was most inconsiderate of the man,' he said to the Muster-Master. 'I do not know whether I ought to proceed to execution, pending his trial for this second murder.'

'Oh,' said the latter functionary – flicking with his handkerchief from his coat-sleeve as he spoke a drop of Convict Glancy's blood that had fallen there from a reflex swirl of the lash, 'I think your duty is clear. You must hang him at nine o'clock, and try him afterwards for the last crime.'

And as Convict Glancy, per Pestonjee Bomanjee (second), No. 17,927, was punctually hanged at 9.5, it is to be presumed that the Under-Sheriff had accepted this solution of the difficulty.

At 10.15 a mass of carrion having been huddled into a shell, and certain formalities, which in the estimation of the System served as efficiently as a coroner's inquest, having been duly attended to, Muster-Master Stoneman bethought himself that he had not breakfasted.

290 *sensibility* (hier) Verstand
291 *hangman* executioner who hangs people
292 *gashed* cut open
292 *coarse* rough
293 *sonny* (infml) young boy
295 *apprise sb.* inform sb.
297 *javelin-man* bewaffneter Gerichtsdiener
301 *pending* while waiting for sth. to happen
304 *swirl* Wirbel
306 *try sb.* put sb. on trial
307 *per* (Latin) using
311 *carrion* decaying flesh of dead animals
311 *huddle sth.* push sth. together
312 *shell* protective case used as a coffin
313 *coroner* official who holds inquests into deaths
314 *attend to sth.* deal with sth.
314 *bethink* (fml) come to think

'I'll see you later, Mr. Ropewell,' he said, as the latter was endorsing the Governor's warrant with the sham verdict; 'I'm going to breakfast. I think I've earned it this morning.'

317 *endorse sth.* (here) officially fill sth. out
317 *sham* not genuine
317 *verdict* Urteil

Tasks

1 Summarize the story in your own words.

2 Examine what view of Christianity comes across in the story.

3 a) Find examples of irony in the story.
b) Explain what the use of ironic statements reveals about the author's attitude towards the convict system.

4 Comment on the following actions in the story:
a) Convict Glancy killing two people and spitting on the dead overseer's grave;
b) Muster-Master Stoneman's double punishment of Glancy.

5 Research information on the convict system in Australia.

Additional Text: Egalitarianism in Australia

This text from the website of Convict Creations examines how its convict past may have influenced Australian society today.

It would be fair to say that Australia is one of the most egalitarian nations in the world. While many countries celebrate the ideal of human equality, arguably none has it so culturally engrained as Australia. The ideological bias towards equality is most clearly seen in the language that Australians use to communicate with each other. In comparison to other English speakers, Australians tend to be far more informal; readily using the same language when dealing with a boss, an elderly person, friend or scallywag. In a famous example, when cricketer Dennis Lillee met the Queen, he greeted her with a handshake and a friendly 'g'day, how ya go'in'.

To outsiders, the egalitarian nature of Australian speech has been seen as a sign of rudeness because it means treating someone of high status in the same manner as a shoe salesman or garbage collector. For example, in 1980, a Japanese prefecture sponsored a weekend seminar to discuss problems that Japanese people might experience in Australia. One speaker, Hiro Mukai, stated: 'Australians appear very naive to the newly-arrived Japanese. They speak the same way with everyone.'

Australia has forged egalitarian sentiments largely because, in its founding era, the authorities were obsessive in depriving convicts and their descendants of it. The convict system ensured that people in positions of superiority were rarely representative of the material, or spiritual, aspirations of the criminal class that constituted the bulk of the population. A census taken in 1828 found that half the population of NSW were convicts, and that former convicts made up nearly half of the free population. Yet despite being in numerical dominance, the convict class was unable to aspire to civic positions that were reserved for the Exclusives (immigrants not of convict stock.) The Exclusives argued against the convict class gaining equal rights on the grounds it would be 'rewarding criminality'. The denial of equality was also extended to the Convict offspring on the grounds the child of a convict would show 'the same proclivity to crime as their parents had deemed to have shown'.

As well as being excluded from holding official positions, the convict class was discriminated against in the distribution of land grants. Whereas free immigrants were frequently given grants running in thousands of acres, convicts were only granted forty

- *egalitarianism* equality

3 *engrained* firmly fixed or established
4 *bias* ['baɪəs] strong feeling for or against sb./sth.
8 *scallywag* person who behaves badly
9 *Dennis Lillee* (born 1949) member of Australian cricket team in the 1970s and 80s
15 *prefecture* ['pri:fektʃə] administrative district
20 *forge sth.* create sth. that is strong
20 *sentiment* feeling
22 *descendant* Nachkomme
24 *aspiration* hope, ambition
26 *NSW* = state of New South Wales
30 *stock* background
34 *proclivity* tendency to do sth. or to feel sth.

acres whilst the native born of convict stock were only allowed sixty acres.

Aside from hating notions of superiority due to conflicts with the Exclusives, the convicts hated notions of superiority due to conflicts amongst themselves. The penal system often elevated one convict to a position of overseer who could then order, or flog, his former friends. J.F Mortlock, an educated convict sent to Australia, wrote about how one convict accepting superiority over another became a violation of etiquette: 'Men betraying their companions or accepting authority over them, are often called "dogs", and sometimes have their noses bitten off – the morsel being termed 'a mouthful of a dog's nose.'

[...] With time, the Convict class came to see their egalitarianism as a social attribute that gave them superiority over the Exclusives. While they might not have had power, education, or wealth, they had a belief in the equality of humanity and this was their strength. A newspaper report explaining: 'Historically, the greatest rift has been between the "exclusives" and the "emancipists". The first group believe that anyone who has come to the colony in penal servitude is never capable of complete redemption. These people, who tend to be among the wealthy landowners, thus see themselves as a superior class. For their part, the emancipists, who are all ex-convicts, are concerned with equality of human rights.'

It seems the values of the convicts won out in the end because the ideal of egalitarianism came to be seen as definitive of Australia values. Just as the ideal of egalitarianism helped the convict class gain a sense of superiority over the Exclusives, subsequent generations used the ideal to ironically express their superiority over other nations. During World War I and II, it was the English who were perceived to be inferior due to their notions of superiority. A commentator, Chester Wilmont, writing: 'They had been taught by their parents, or had otherwise acquired, a strong dislike of the speech, manners and attitudes of the higher British classes. It was possibly the latter's nonchalant sense of superiority, combined with a lack of sensitivity to the suffering of the troops, that infuriated the ANZACs most.'

50 *morsel* small amount or piece
59 *redemption* the act of saving or being saved from the power of evil
67 *subsequent* happening or coming after sth. else
74 *nonchalant* ['nɒnʃələnt] casually calm and relaxed
76 *ANZAC* soldier in the Australian and New Zealand Army Corps

Tasks

1 Outline the influence of Australia's convict past on the country's society.

2 List the examples given in the text where this influence becomes apparent.

3 Explain the Australian attitude towards the British as discussed in the text.

4 Compare German and Australian attitudes to social equality.

HENRY LAWSON **The Drover's Wife**

Henry Lawson (1867–1922) was a writer of short stories and ballads. He was born in Grenfell, New South Wales. His father was a Norwegian immigrant and his mother a leading Australian suffragette. Lawson suffered an ear infection when he was a boy and by the time he was 14 he was completely deaf. As a writer and journalist he focused on politics and social issues and became a convinced republican who spoke out for more independence from Britain. After a trip to the outback he started to write several stories about the hardships and bleakness of the remote life in the Australian bush. At the end of his life Lawson became entirely withdrawn from Australian public life, developed an alcohol addiction and did not manage to maintain his high standard of writing. He died in Sydney in 1922.

Due to low rainfall and infertile soil, the Australian bush is relatively sparsely settled, and the land is mostly used for sheep rearing. However, the history of its exploration and settlement provides Australians with a culturally unique identity. In Henry Lawson's 'The Drover's Wife' the reader gets an impression of the life of women in the early days of outback settlement. The story was written in 1892 and is often considered to be one of the first accurate descriptions of Australian life in the bush.

The two-roomed house is built of round timber, slabs, and stringy bark, and floored with split slabs. A big bark kitchen standing at one end is larger than the house itself, verandah included.

Bush all round – bush with no horizon, for the country is flat. No ranges in the distance. The bush consists of stunted, rotten native apple trees. No undergrowth. Nothing to relieve the eye save the darker green of a few sheoaks which are sighing above the narrow, almost waterless creek. Nineteen miles to the nearest sign of civilisation – a shanty on the main road.

The drover, an ex-squatter, is away with sheep. His wife and children are left here alone.

Four ragged, dried-up-looking children are playing about the house. Suddenly one of them yells: 'Snake! Mother, here's a snake!'

The gaunt, sun-browned bushwoman dashes from the kitchen, snatches her baby from the ground, holds it on her left hip, and reaches for a stick.

'Where is it?'

• *drover* person who moves cows or sheep from one place to another
1 *timber* wood prepared for use in buildings
1 *slab* flat piece of wood
2 *stringy bark* eucalyptus tree
6 *range* Hügelkette
6 *stunted* (adj) not grown or developed as much as it should have
7 *undergrowth* Dickicht, Gestrüpp
7 *relieve sth.* remove an unpleasant feeling from sth.
8 *save* except
8 *sheoak* type of Australian tree
9 *creek* (AustEng) small river
10 *shanty* Bretterbude, Hütte
12 *squatter* (in Australia) settler who occupied land which they did not own in order to keep cattle or sheep
14 *ragged* wearing old and torn clothes
17 *gaunt* [gɔːnt] very thin, usu. because of illness, worry or lack of food
17 *bushwoman* woman who lives in the bush
17 *dash* run in a great hurry

'Here! Gone into the wood-heap!' yells the eldest boy – a sharp-faced, excited urchin of eleven. 'Stop there, mother! I'll have him. Stand back! I'll have the beggar!'

'Tommy, come here, or you'll be bit. Come here at once when I tell you, you little wretch!'

The youngster comes reluctantly, carrying a stick bigger than himself. Then he yells, triumphantly:

'There it goes – under the house!' and darts away with club uplifted.

At the same time the big, black, yellow-eyed dog of all breeds, who has shown the wildest interest in the proceedings, breaks his chain and rushes after that snake. He is a moment late, however, and his nose reaches the crack in the slabs just as the end of its tails disappears. Almost at the same moment the boy's club comes down and skins the aforesaid nose. Alligator takes small notice of this, and proceeds to undermine the building; but he is subdued after a struggle and chained up. They cannot afford to lose him.

The drover's wife makes the children stand together near the doghouse while she watches for the snake. She gets two small dishes of milk and sets them down near the wall to tempt it to come out; but an hour goes by and it does not show itself.

It is near sunset, and a thunderstorm is coming. The children must be brought inside. She will not take them into the house, for she knows the snake is there, and may at any moment come up through the cracks in the rough slab floor; so she carries several armfuls of firewood into the kitchen, and then takes the children there. The kitchen has no floor – or, rather, an earthen one – called a 'ground floor' in this part of the bush. There is a large, roughly made table in the centre of the place. She brings the children in, and makes them get on this table. They are two boys and two girls – mere babies. She gives them some supper, and then, before it gets dark, she goes into the house, and snatches up some pillows and bedclothes – expecting to see or lay her hand on the snake any minute. She makes a bed on the kitchen table for the children, and sits down beside it to watch all night.

She has an eye on the corner, and a green sapling club laid in readiness on the dresser by her side, together with her sewing basket and a copy of the *Young Ladies' Journal*. She has brought the dog into the room.

Tommy turns in, under protest, but says he'll lie awake all night and smash that blinded snake.

His mother asks him how many times she has told him not to swear.

22 *urchin* child who is poorly dressed
25 *wretch* (here) person who behaves badly
26 *reluctant* unwilling
29 *club* heavy stick with a thick end
30 *dog of all breeds* Köter
31 *proceedings* (pl) events
35 *skin sth.* remove the skin from sth.
36 *aforesaid* that has just been mentioned
36 *proceed* continue
37 *undermine sth.* dig under sth.
50 *earthen* made of compressed earth
53 *mere* nur, nichts als
59 *sapling* young tree
60 *dresser* sideboard with shelves for plates
63 *turn in* (infml) go to bed

He has his club with him under the bedclothes, and Jacky protests:

'Mummy! Tommy's skinnin' me alive wif his club. Make him take it out.'

Tommy: 'Shet up, you little –! D'yer want to be bit with the snake?'

Jacky shuts up.

'If yer bit,' says Tommy, after a pause, 'you'll swell up, an' smell, an' turn red an' green an' blue all over till yer bust. Won't he, mother?'

'Now then, don't frighten the child. Go to sleep,' she says.

The two younger children go to sleep, and now and then Jacky complains of being 'skeezed'. More room is made for him. Presently Tommy says: 'Mother! Listen to them (adjective) little 'possums. I'd like to screw their blanky necks.'

And Jacky protests drowsily:

'But they don't hurt us, the little blanks!'

Mother: 'There, I told you you'd teach Jacky to swear.' But the remark makes her smile. Jacky goes to sleep.

Presently Tommy asks:

'Mother! Do you think they'll ever extricate the (adjective) kangaroo?'

'Lord! How am I to know, child? Go to sleep.'

'Will you wake me if the snake comes out?'

'Yes. Got to sleep.'

Near midnight. The children are all asleep and she sits there still, sewing and reading by turns. From time to time she glances round the floor and wall-plate, and whenever she hears a noise she reaches for the stick. The thunderstorm

71 *d'yer* do you
75 *bust* (here) die
80 *skeez* = squeeze
81 *(adjective)* used to show that a swear word was used
82 *'possum* = *Opossum* australische Beutelratte
82 *blanky* word used to avoid writing a swear word
83 *drowsy* sleepy and lethargic
88 *extricate sth.* free sth. from a difficulty
95 *wall-plate* Stützbalken

Infobox | The Bush

The Australian bush has an iconic status in Australian life and features strongly in any discussion about national identity. The Australian bush is the term given to the territory beyond the fertile coast areas of Australia – the landscape usually contains woody shrubs and bushes with certain types of trees, especially eucalyptus trees, scattered around. The bush was something that was uniquely Australian and very different to the green landscapes familiar to European immigrants. In early Australian history, living outside the confines of civilization was sometimes seen as a preferred option to the harsh conditions experienced by convicts. Since then the bush has evoked themes of struggle and survival, in which a harsh landscape forms a resourceful, independent and tough character.

comes on, and the wind, rushing through the cracks in the slab wall, threatens to blow out her candle. She places it on a sheltered part of the dresser and fixes up a newspaper to protect it. At every flash of lightning, the cracks between the slabs gleam like polishes silver. The thunder rolls, and the rain comes down in torrents.

Alligator lies at full length on the floor, with his eyes turned towards the partition. She knows by this that the snake is there. There are large cracks in that wall opening under the floor of the dwelling-house.

She is not a coward, but recent events have shaken her nerves. A little son of her brother-in-law was lately bitten by a snake, and died. Besides, she has not heard from her husband for six months, and is anxious about him.

He was a drover, and started squatting here when they were married.

The drought of 18– ruined him. He had to sacrifice the remnant of his flock and go droving again. He intends to move his family into the nearest town when he comes back, and, in the meantime, his brother, who keeps a shanty on the main road, comes over about once a month with provisions. The wife has still a couple of cows, one horse, and a few sheep. The brother-in-law kills one of the sheep occasionally, gives her what she needs of it, and takes the rest in return for other provisions.

She is used to being left alone. She once lived like this for eighteen months. As a girl she built the usual castles in the air; but all her girlish hopes and aspirations have long been dead. She finds all the excitement and recreation she needs in the *Young Ladies' Journal*, and, Heaven help her! takes a pleasure in the fashion-plates.

Her husband is an Australian, and so is she. He is careless, but a good enough husband. If he had the means he would take her to the city and keep her there like a princess. They are used to being apart, or at least she is. 'No use fretting,' she says. He may forget sometimes that he is married; but if he has a good cheque when he comes back he will give most of it to her. When he had money he took her to the city several times – hired a railway sleeping compartment, and put up at the best hotels. He also bought her a buggy, but they had to sacrifice that along with the rest.

The last two children were born in the bush – one while her husband was bringing a drunken doctor, by force, to attend to her. She was alone on this occasion, and very weak. She had been ill with a fever. She prayed to God to send her assistance. God sent Black Mary – the 'whitest' gin in all the land. Or, at least, God sent 'King Jimmy' first, and he sent

102 *torrent* large amount
104 *partition* Trennwand
111 *squat* (AustEng) keep cattle or sheep on land that is not legally your own
113 *drought* [draʊt] Dürre
114 *remnant* small remaining part
117 *provisions* (pl) supplies of food and drink
123 *build castles in the air* have dreams of a better life
124 *aspiration* strong desire to have or do sth.
127 *fashion-plate* picture of fashionable clothes
131 *fret* be constantly anxious
136 *buggy* horse-drawn vehicle for one or two people
139 *attend to sb.* (of a doctor) look after sb.
142 *white* (AustEng) decent
142 *gin* (AustEng, old use) Aboriginal woman

Black Mary. He put his black face round the door-post, took in the situation at a glance, and said cheerfully: 'All right, Missis – I bring my old woman, she down alonga creek.'

One of her children died while she was here alone. She rode nineteen miles for assistance, carrying the dead child.

It must be near one or two o'clock. The fire is burning low. Alligator lies with his head resting on his paws, and watches the wall. He is not a very beautiful dog to look at, and the light shows numerous old wounds where the hair will not grow. He is afraid of nothing on the face of the earth or under it. He will tackle a bullock as readily as he will tackle a flea. He hates all other dogs – except kangaroo-dogs – and has a marked dislike to friends or relations of the family. They seldom call, however. He sometimes makes friends with strangers. He hates snakes and has killed many, but he will be bitten some day and die; most snake-dogs end that way.

Now and then the bushwoman lays down her work and watches, and listens, and thinks. She thinks of things in her own life, for there is little else to think about.

The rain will make the grass grow, and this reminds her how she fought a bush fire once while her husband was away. The grass was long, and very dry, and the fire threatened to burn her out. She put on an old pair of her husband's trousers and beat out the flames with a green bough, till great drops of sooty perspiration stood out on her forehead and ran in streaks down her blackened arms. The sight of his mother in trousers greatly amused Tommy, who worked like a little hero by her side, but the terrified baby howled lustily for his 'mummy'. The fire would have mastered her but for four excited bushmen who arrived in the nick of time. It was a mixed-up affair all round; when she went to take up the baby he screamed and struggled convulsively, thinking it was a 'black man'; and Alligator, trusting more to the child's sense than his own instinct, charged furiously, and (being old and slightly deaf) did not in his excitement at first recognise his mistress's voice, but continued to hang on to the moleskins until choked off by Tommy with a saddle-strap. The dog's sorrow for his blunder, and his anxiety to let it be known that it was all a mistake, was as evident as his ragged tail and a twelve-inch grin could make it. It was a glorious time for the boys; a day to look back to, and talk about, and laugh over for many years.

She thinks how she fought a flood during her husband's absence. She stood for hours in the drenching downpour, and dug an overflow gutter to save the dam across the creek.

146 *alonga* (dialect) along the
154 *bullock* Ochse
155 *kangaroo-dog* type of dog used for hunting
156 *marked* clear, noticeable
168 *bough* [baʊ] branch
169 *sooty* rußig
169 *perspiration* Schweiß, Transpiration
172 *howl* cry like a dog
173 *but for ...* if it had not been for ...
174 *bushman* man who lives in the bush
174 *in the nick of time* just before sth. happens, just in time
176 *convulsively* krampfartig
181 *moleskin* type of strong cotton cloth
181 *choke sb./sth.* strangle sb/sth.
182 *blunder* mistake
188 *drench sb./sth.* make sb./sth. completely wet
189 *gutter* Gosse, Rinne

Typical houses in the bush in the 19th century. This photo shows Henry Lawson's mother and his brother.

But she could not save it. There are things that a bushwoman cannot do. Next morning the dam was broken, and her heart was nearly broken too, for she thought how her husband would feel when he came home and saw the result of years of labour swept away. She cried then.

She also fought the *pleuro-pneumonia* – dosed and bled the few remaining cattle, and wept again when her two best cows died.

Again, she fought a mad bullock that besieged the house for a day. She made bullets and fired at him through cracks in the slabs with an old shotgun. He was dead in the morning. She skinned him and got seventeen and six for the hide.

She also fights the crows and eagles that have designs on her chickens. Her plan of campaign is very original. The children cry 'Crows, mother!' and she rushes out and aims a broomstick at the birds as though it were a gun, and says, 'Bung!' The crows leave in a hurry; they are cunning, but a woman's cunning is greater.

Occasionally a bushman in the horrors, or a villainous-looking sundowner, comes and nearly scares the life out of her. She generally tells the suspicious-looking stranger that her husband and two sons are at work below the dam, or over at the yard, for he always cunningly enquires for the boss.

195 *pleuro-pneumonia* [ˌplʊərəʊnjuː'məʊniə] type of pneumonia (= Lungenentzündung) that affects cattle
195 *bleed sb./sth.* (old use) take blood from sb./sth. as a way of treating a disease
198 *besiege sth.* surround sth. (usu. a place) and attack it
201 *seventeen and six* seventeen shillings and six pence (i.e. nearly a pound)
201 *hide* skin of an animal
208 *in the horrors* (infml) very drunk
208 *villainous* ['vɪlənəs] evil
209 *sundowner* (AustEng) man who travels around the country pretending to be looking for work

Only last week a gallows-faced swagman – having satisfied himself that there were no men on the place – threw his swag down on the verandah, and demanded tucker. She gave him something to eat; then he expressed his intention of staying for the night. It was sundown then. She got a batten from the sofa, loosened the dog, and confronted the stranger, holding the batten in one hand and the dog's collar with the other. 'Now you go!' she said. He looked at her and at the dog, said 'All right, mum,' in a cringing tone, and left. She was a determined-looking woman, and Alligator's yellow eyes glared unpleasantly – besides, the dog's chawing-up apparatus greatly resembled that of the reptile he was named after.

She has few pleasures to think of as she sits here alone by the fire, on guard against a snake. All days are much the same to her, but on Sunday afternoon she dresses herself, tidies the children, smartens up baby, and goes for a lonely walk along the bush-track, pushing an old perambulator in front of her. She does this every Sunday. She takes as much care to make herself and the children look smart as she would if she were going to do the block in the city. There is nothing to see, however, and not a soul to meet. You might walk for twenty miles along this track without being able to fix a point in your mind, unless you are a bushman. This is because of the everlasting, maddening sameness of the stunted trees – that monotony which makes a man long to break away and travel as far as trains can go, and sail as far a ships can sail – and further.

But this bushwoman is used to the loneliness of it. As a girl-wife she hated it, but now she would feel strange away from it.

She is glad when her husband returns, but she does not gush or make a fuss about it. She gets him something good to eat, and tidies up the children.

She seems contented with her lot. She loves her children, but has no time to show it. She seems harsh to them. Her surroundings are not favourable to the development of the 'womanly' or sentimental side of nature.

It must be near morning now; but the clock is in the dwelling-house. Her candle is nearly done; she forgot that she was out of candles. Some more wood must be got to keep the fire up, and so she shuts the dog inside and hurries round to the wood-heap. The rain has cleared off. She seized a stick, pulls it out, and – crash! the whole pile collapses.

Yesterday she bargained with a stray blackfellow to bring her some wood, and while he was at work she went in search

214 *gallows* (pl) structure on which people were killed by hanging
214 *swagman* (AustEng) man who travels around looking for work
216 *swag* bundle of things tied or wrapped together
216 *tucker* (AustEng infml) food
218 *batten* Latte, Leiste
224 *chaw* chew
231 *perambulator* (old use) Kinderwagen
234 *do the block* eine Runde um den Block drehen
246 *gush* show too much emotion
248 *contented* feeling happiness
248 *lot* fate, position in life
258 *bargain* discuss a price
258 *stray* by himself, alone

of a missing cow. She was absent an hour or so, and the native black made good use of his time. On her return she was so astonished to see a good heap of wood by the chimney, that she gave him an extra fig of tobacco, and praised him for not being lazy. He thanked her, and left with head erect and chest well out. He was the last of his tribe and a King; but he had built that wood-heap hollow.

She is hurt now, and tears spring to her eyes as she sits down again by the table. She takes up a handkerchief to wipe the tears away, but pokes her eyes with her bare fingers instead. The handkerchief is full of holes, and she finds that she has put her thumb through one, and her forefinger through another.

This makes her laugh, to the surprise of the dog. She has a keen, very keen, sense of the ridiculous; and some time or other she will amuse bushmen with the story.

She has been amused before like that. One day she sat down 'to have a good cry,' as she said – and the old cat rubbed against her dress and 'cried too'. Then she had to laugh.

It must be near daylight. The room is very close and hot because of the fire. Alligator still watches the wall from time to time. Suddenly he becomes greatly interested; he draws himself a few inches nearer the partition, and a thrill runs through his body. The hair on the back of his neck begins to bristle, and the battle-light is in his yellow eyes. She knows what this means, and lays her hand on the stick. The lower end of one of the partition slabs has a large crack on both sides. An evil pair of small, bright, bead-like eyes glisten at one of these holes. The snake – a black one – comes slowly out, about a foot, and moves its head up and down. The dog lies still, and the woman sits as one fascinated. The snake comes out a foot further. She lifts her stick, and the reptile, as though suddenly aware of danger, sticks his head in through the crack on the other side of the slab, and hurries to get his tail round after him. Alligator springs, and his jaws come together with a snap. He misses, for his nose is large and the snake's body close down in the angle formed by the slabs and the floor. He snaps again as the tail comes round. He has the snake now, and tugs it out eighteen inches. Thud, thud comes the woman's club on the ground. Alligator pulls again. Thud, thud. Alligator gives another pull and he has the snake out – a black brute, five feet long. The head rises to dart about, but the dog has the enemy close to the neck. He is a big, heavy dog, but quick as a terrier. He shakes the snake as though he felt the original curse in common with mankind. The eldest boy wakes up, seizes his stick, and tries

263 *fig* (here) small piece of tobacco
274 *keen* sharp
284 *bristle* ['brɪsl] (of hair) stand upright away from the skin
298 *tug sth. out* pull sth. out
304 *the original curse* God's curse that made the snake an enemy of mankind after Adam and Eve listened to the snake and not to God

to get out of bed, but his mother forces him back with a grip of iron. Thud, thud – the snake's back is broken in several places. Thud, thud – its head is crushed, and Alligator's nose skinned again.

She lifts the mangled reptile on the point of her stick, carries it to the fire, and throws it in; then piles on the wood, and watches the snake burn. The boy and dog watch, too. She lays her hand on the dog's head, and all the fierce, angry light dies out of his yellow eyes. The younger children are quieted, and presently go to sleep. The dirty-legged boy stands for a moment in his shirt, watching the fire. Presently he looks up at her, sees the tears in her eyes, and throwing his arms round her neck, exclaims:

'Mother, I won't never go drovin'; blast me if I do!'

And she hugs him to her worn-out breast and kisses him; and they sit thus together while the sickly daylight breaks over the bush.

310 *mangle sth.* damage sth. by tearing or crushing it

Tasks

1 Describe how Lawson characterizes the landscape.

2 Examine the effect of the country and nature on the life of the drover's family.

3 Analyse Henry Lawson's mode of presentation in this short story.

4 Write short character descriptions of a) the drover's wife and b) Thommy.

5 Using information from task 4, describe the situation of women in the early days of farming in the outback.

6 Examine the relationship between the family and other people, and point out to what extent it is a result of life in the bush.

7 Write a letter to a friend in which the drover's wife expresses her longing for a life in a more civilized environment.

Additional Text:
Eric Bogle Now I'm Easy

For nearly sixty years, I've been a Cockie
Of droughts and fires and floods I've lived through plenty
This country's dust and mud have seen my tears and blood
But it's nearly over now, and now I'm easy

I married a fine girl when I was twenty
But she died in giving birth when she was thirty
No flying doctor then, just a gentle old black gin
But it's nearly over now, and now I'm easy

She left me with two sons and a daughter
And a bone-dry farm whose soil cried out for water
So my care was rough and ready but they grew up fine and steady
But it's nearly over now, and now I'm easy

My daughter married young, and went her own way
My sons lie buried by the Burma Railway
So on this land I've made me home I've carried on alone
But it's nearly over now, and now I'm easy

City folks these days despise the Cockie
Say with subsidies and dole, we've had it easy
But there's no drought or starving stock on a sewered suburban block
But it's nearly over now, and now I'm easy

For nearly sixty years, I've been a Cockie
Of droughts and fires and floods I've lived through plenty
This country's dust and mud have seen my tears and blood
But it's nearly over now, and now I'm easy

***From:** the website of Eric Bogle, 1997*

1 *Cockie* (AustEng infml) outback farmer
7 *flying doctor* airborne emergency and health care service for people living in rural, remote and regional areas of Australia.
10 *bone-dry* extremely dry
10 *soil* earth in which plants grow
14 *Burma Railway* railway built by Japan during World War II. More than 2800 Australian prisoners of war who were used as forced labourers died in its construction.
17 *city folks* people living in a city
18 *subsidy* money paid by a government or an organization to reduce the costs of producing goods
18 *dole* (infml) unemployment benefit
19 *sewered* [ˌsuːərd] an den öffentlichen Schmutzwasserkanal angeschlossen

Tasks

1. Explain why the Cockie is 'easy' at the end of his life.
2. Comment on the opinion of city folks in the fifth stanza.
3. Write a dialogue between the Cockie and the drover's wife in which they reflect on their life, their hopes and disappointments.

Additional Text:
D.H. Lawrence Openness and Freedom

In this passage from D.H. Lawrence's novel Kangaroo *(1923), the English protagonist Somers considers his reaction to Australia, a country he has just recently arrived in.*

This was Sunday afternoon. The sun was warm. The lonely man was just pushing off his boat on the lagoon. It sat deep in the water, half full of sand. Somers and Harriet lay on the sand-bank. Strange it was. And it HAD a sort of fascination. Freedom! That's what they always say. 'You feel free in Australia.' And so you do. There is a great relief in the atmosphere, a relief from tension, from pressure. An absence of control or will or form. The sky is open above you, and the air is open around you. Not the old closing-in of Europe.

But what then? The VACANCY of this freedom is almost terrifying. In the openness and the freedom this new chaos, this litter of bungalows and tin cans scattered for miles and miles, this Englishness all crumbled out into formlessness and chaos. Even the heart of Sydney itself – an imitation of London and New York, without any core or pith of meaning. Business going on full speed: but only because it is the other end of English and American business.

The absence of any inner meaning: and at the same time the great sense of vacant spaces. The sense of irresponsible freedom. The sense of do-as-you-please liberty. And all utterly uninteresting. What is more hopelessly uninteresting than accomplished liberty? Great swarming, teeming Sydney flowing out into these myriads of bungalows, like shallow waters spreading, undyked. And what then? Nothing. No inner life, no high command, no interest in anything, finally.

Somers turned over and shut his eyes. New countries were more problematic than old ones. One loved the sense of release from old pressure and old tight control, from the old world of water-tight compartments. This was Sunday afternoon, but with none of the surfeited dreariness of English Sunday afternoons. It was still a raw loose world. All Sydney would be out by the sea or in the bush, a roving, unbroken world. They all rushed from where they were to somewhere else, on holidays. And tomorrow they'd all be working away, with just as little meaning, working without any meaning, playing without any meaning; and yet quite strenuous at it all. It was just dazing. Even the rush for money had no real pip in it. They really cared very little for the power that money can give. And except for the sense of power, that had no

2 *lagoon* small lake, usu. with salt water
6 *relief* Erleichterung, Entlastung
11 *litter* rubbish that is scattered around
12 *tin can* (here) small house made mostly of metal
15 *core, pith* Kern
22 *swarming, teeming* full of people
23 *myriad* ['mɪriəd] large number
23 *undyked* [ʌn'daɪkd] with no dykes (= Deiche) to control the movement
30 *surfeited* having had too much of sth.
30 *dreariness* Eintönigkeit
32 *roving* travelling around
36 *strenuous* anstrengend
37 *pip* (here) excitement

real significance here. When all is said and done, even money is not much good where there is no genuine culture. Money is a means to rising to a higher, subtler, fuller state of consciousness, or nothing. And when you flatly don't want a fuller consciousness, what good is your money to you? Just to chuck about and gamble with. Even money is a European invention – European and American. It has no real magic in Australia.

***From:** D.H. Lawrence,* Kangaroo, *London: William Heinemann, 1923*

Tasks

1 Compare the differences between Australia and Europe as described in the passage.

2 Imagine the drover's wife read this passage from the novel. How might she react to it?

KATHARINE SUSANNAH PRICHARD **Marlene**

Katharine Susannah Prichard (1883–1969) was a writer and political activist. She was born in Fiji but spent her childhood in Tasmania before moving with her family to Melbourne. Unlike her brother, she was not sent to a university but was able to get access to literature by visiting the Melbourne Public Library. As a governess, Prichard began her lifelong practice of noting down detailed accounts of people and places that would recur in her fiction. Following her marriage in 1920 she moved to Perth, Western Australia, where she lived for the rest of her life. Prichard was a founding member of the Communist Party of Australia in 1921 and remained a member until her death. Much of her fiction deals with the living conditions of the working classes, e.g. *Working Bullocks* (1926), which portrays the physical and emotional damage done to timber workers, and *The Goldfields Trilogy* (1946–1950), which gives an insight into the working conditions in Western Australia's goldmines. In her novel *Coonardoo* (1929) she deals with the relationship between white men and Aboriginal women in the north-west of Australia.

In her short story 'Marlene' (first published 1938) Prichard depicts the situation of so-called 'half-castes' and the relationship between Europeans and non-Europeans.

Coming out from the trees, the camp on the hillside was almost invisible. It crouched among rocks and wet undergrowth, with the township lying under mists in the valley below. The wurlies of bark, bagging and matted leaves had taken on the colouring of the rocks and tree-trunks. They were shaped like mounds of earth: crude shells with open mouths. A breath of smoke betrayed them. It hung in the air and drifted away among the trees.

Two women riding along the bush track detected the first humpy, then another and another, until half a dozen were in sight about a rough open space. Dogs flew out, barking fiercely. Two or three children, barelegged, lean, sallow, bright-eyed, with black tousled hair, slid out from before the wurlies. A man lying beside a fire sat up and glanced at the women.

'Hullo, Benjy,' the elderly woman on a grey horse called. 'Sleeping in this morning? Where's Mollie?'

The man grunted, starting sullenly over the rain-sodden clearing. Men and women appeared at the open mouths of other wurlies, all dressed as they had been sleeping, in faded dungarees and khaki trousers, shirts and skirts grey with

1 *camp* Aboriginal settlement
2 *crouch* kauern, hocken
2 *undergrowth* Dickicht
3 *township* small town
4 *wurlie/wurley* (AustEng) simple Aboriginal temporary shelter
4 *bark* outer covering of a tree
4 *bagging* cloth
4 *matted* (here) pressed together
6 *mound* small hill
6 *crude* rough, primitive
7 *betray sth.* reveal sth.
10 *humpy* (AustEng) simple Aboriginal temporary shelter
12 *barelegged* wearing no clothes on the legs or feet
12 *lean* (of a person) thin
12 *sallow* (of a person's face) yellowish or pale brown
13 *bright-eyed* alert and lively
13 *tousled* ['taʊzld] untidy
13 *slide* move quickly along a smooth surface
18 *sullen* bad-tempered and sulky
18 *sodden* very wet
19 *clearing* open space in a forest
21 *dungarees* [ˌdʌŋgə'riːz] trousers held up by straps over the shoulders

grime and grease, threadbare woollen jackets and coats – cast-off clothing of the townspeople.

'Hullo, Mrs Boyd,' some of the women called.

'This is Miss Cecily Allison,' Mrs Boyd explained, introducing the girl on the chestnut colt. 'Miss Allison's from England; going to write a book about the aborigines. She wanted to see your camp.'

'We're half-castes here – not abos,' a morose, middle-aged man replied.

'And not "at home" so early in the day,' one of the young men added sarcastically. 'It's a hell of a place to see, anyhow.'

'Y're fergettin' y'r manners, Albert – swearin' before ladies!' one of the women said.

She giggled shyly.

A traditional wurley or humpey

'How's yerself, Mrs Boyd?'

'I'm well, Tilly. But you're looking like drowned rats, the lot of you. Why don't you shift camp for the winter, George?'

Mrs Boyd sat her upstanding mount squarely, as well-conditioned as he was. A good horsewoman, capable of managing her own affairs, it was evident. Her manner was authoritative, but kind and friendly.

'Where'd we shift to?' a fat, youngish woman asked jocosely. Barefooted, she stood, a once-white dress dragged across her heavy breast and thighs, a youngster slung on one hip. A little laugh nibbled its way through the crowd.

'This is the only place we're allowed to camp in the district,' the man who had first spoken said sourly. 'You know that, Mrs Boyd.'

'The rain's been comin' down steady for two months.' One of the other women raised a flat, uncomplaining treble.

'How on earth do you manage to get a dry spot in the humpies or keep your clothes dry?'

'We don't.' The crowd laughed as though that were a good joke. 'Our clothes are all soakin'. There's not a dry blanket in the camp.'

'We ought to be ducks. The rain'd run off our backs then.'

'It's a disgrace you should have to live like this,' Mrs Boyd declared. 'But what I came about this morning is Mollie. Where is she?'

The crowd shifted uneasily. Eyes encountered and glanced aside. A wild crew they looked in their shabby

22 *grime* black dirt
22 *grease* Fett
22 *threadbare* worn out
23 *cast-off* not wanted by other people anymore
26 *chestnut* reddish-brown
26 *colt* young male horse
30 *half-caste* person of mixed race
31 *abo* (infml derog) Aborigine
31 *morose* bad-tempered
37 *y're fergettin'* (dialect) you're forgetting
42 *the lot of you* all of you
43 *shift sth.* move sth.
44 *upstanding* strong and healthy
44 *mount* horse used for riding
46 *evident* clear, obvious
48 *jocose* [dʒəˈkəʊs] playful, humorous
50 *thigh* Oberschenkel
50 *slung* (here) hanging
51 *hip* Hüfte
51 *nibble* (here) move through
56 *raise a treble* speak in a high-pitched voice
60 *soakin'* extremely wet
67 *encounter* meet unexpectedly

clothes, the women wearing remnants of finery, a bright scarf or coloured cardigan over their draggled dresses.

Brown-eyed, black-haired, they all were, but their skin varied from sickly yellow to weathered bronze. The women were sallow and tawny, the men darker. On most of the faces, thick noses and full lips denoted the aboriginal strain; a few others had sharp, neat features, showing no trace of aboriginal origin except in their eyes.

'Where is Mollie?' Mrs Boyd demanded. 'I've been letting Mr Edward drive her in to the pictures on Saturday nights when he goes into town himself. But she didn't come back with him last week. He waited an hour for her.'

'She's fair mad about the pictures, Mollie,' Ruby burbled.

'That's all very well, but it's not very considerate of her to run away like this. She knows how busy we are just now with all the cows coming in. Mr Phillip and Mr Edward've got their hands full. I had to ride in with the mail myself this morning. And Mollie was very useful, helping with the milking and feeding poddies.'

'She's a fine kid, Mollie,' Albert declared.

'But where is she? What's the matter?'

The crowd surged. Obviously the question was disturbing: it had to be evaded. Exclamations and suggestions clattered. There was no surprise, no consternation, although everybody seemed upset, a little nervous and amused at Mrs Boyd's query.

Mrs Boyd guessed they were hiding Mollie. The child had got a quirk about something: one of those mysterious urges to go bush with her own kind.

'Did y'know Bill Bibblemun took bad with the p'monia and died in hospital, Sunday week?' somebody asked.

Others joined in eagerly.

'It was a grand funeral, Mrs Boyd.'

'The Salvation Army captain said Bill'd go straight to glory because he was a good Christian.'

'He was, too. Testified at street meetings and sang hymns – even when he was drunk.'

'They said some beautiful prayers.'

'All about his bein' washed in the blood of the lamb and his sins bein' whiter than snow.'

'And the kids have all had measles,' Ruby boasted.

'What's happened to Wally Williams?' Mrs Boyd inquired, willing to humour them. 'He was to come over and cut fencing-posts for me last month.'

69 *remnant* small remaining part of sth.
69 *finery* Pracht
70 *draggle sth.* make sth. wet and dirty
73 *tawny* orange brown
74 *denote sth.* be a sign of sth., indicate sth.
74 *strain* origin
75 *neat* pleasing to look at
81 *be fair mad about sth.* really like sth.
81 *burble* make a murmuring noise
83 *considerate* rücksichtsvoll
88 *poddy* lamb or calf fed by hand
91 *surge* move suddenly
92 *evade sth.* avoid sth.
92 *clatter* make a loud rattling sound
95 *query* question asking for information
97 *quirk* Eigenart, Tick, Marotte
98 *go bush* (AustrEng infml) run wild
99 *take bad* (infml) become ill
99 *p'monia = pneumonia* [njuːˈməʊniə] Lungenentzüdung
100 *Sunday week* the Sunday before the last one
103 *Salvation Army* Heilsarmee
105 *testify* express your belief in God
110 *measles* (pl) Masern
110 *boast* talk with pride and self-satisfaction
113 *fencing post* Zaunpfosten

There was a lull in the rattle of voices, eyelids fell, wary glances slid under them. Coughing, a hoarse whispering, filled the pause.

'He's gone up-country,' George said.

'You mean, he's in jail. What's he been up to now?'

'Well, you see, Mrs Boyd, it wasn't hardly Wally's fault,' Tilly Lewis explained. 'Jo Wiggins said some steers had got out of his holding-paddocks, and he offered Wally two bob for every steer he could track and bring in. Wally took in a couple of cleanskins. He thought they were Mr Wiggins's steers, natcherly –'

'Naturally – at two bob apiece,' Mrs Boyd agreed.

'But when the mounted trooper found a couple of red poley steer skins in Jo Wiggins's slaughteryard, Mr Wiggins put the blame on to Wally – and Wally got two years.'

'Everybody knows Jo Wiggins's game,' Mrs Boyd admitted. 'But Wally ought to keep his hands off cleanskins.'

'Oh, he's not like that, Wally, Mrs Boyd. He's a real good stockman. But if he can't get a job, he doesn't know what to do with hisself. He's jest got to be workin' cattle –'

'I know.' Mrs Boyd laughed good-humouredly. 'I suspect he's "worked" calves from our back hills before now. We had an epidemic of milkers coming in without calves last year.'

'If a cow drops a calf in the bush, Mrs Boyd, the dingoes are as likely to get it as –'

'Wally! Of course. But my money's on Wally. I reckon Jo Wiggins has had more of our calves than the dingoes.'

Her horse, cropping the young grass, swung Mrs Boyd sideways. She saw the figure of a man sleeping before a smouldering fire at the entrance of his shack. Steam was rising from the damp blanket that covered him.

'Who's that?' she asked.

'It's Charley,' a woman who had been coughing incessantly said. 'He's not well.'

'Better put that bottle away then,' Mrs Boyd advised. 'If the trooper comes round somebody'll be getting into trouble for selling Charley plonk again. Where does he get the money to buy drink, anyhow?'

'The shopkeepers take his drawings for showcards sometimes.'

'He's quite an artist in his own way, Charley,' Mrs Boyd explained to her companion. 'Self-taught. Could you show Miss Allison some of Charley's drawings, Lizzie?'

Charley's wife slipped away, burrowed into the wurley, and returned with a black exercise-book in her hands. Miss

114 *lull* period of quiet or inactivity
114 *wary* careful when dealing with sb.
115 *hoarse* rough and harsh
117 *up-country* inland
120 *steer* castrated bull
121 *holding-paddock* enclosed small piece of land
121 *bob* (former British currency) shilling
123 *cleanskin* unbranded animal
124 *natcherly* (dialect) naturally
126 *mounted trooper* policeman on a horse
127 *poley* (AustrEng) cow without horns
132 *stockman* Australian cowboy
133 *hisself* (dialect) himself
133 *jest* (dialect) just
136 *epidemic* bad thing that happens in a large number
136 *milker* cow kept for milk
138 *drop sth.* (infml) give birth to sth.
140 *my money's on Wally* I think Wally did it
140 *reckon* (infml) think, suppose
142 *crop sth.* eat the top of sth.
144 *smouldering* burning slowly with smoke but no flame
144 *shack* roughly built hut or cabin
147 *incessant* continuing without interruption
151 *plonk* (infml) cheap wine
153 *showcard* form of advertisement in shop windows

Allison dismounted to look at the drawings, crude outlines of people and animals, a football match, the finish of a race.

Pleasure in Charley's drawings, awed interest and expectancy animated his friends and relations.

'Well' – Mrs Boyd yanked her horse's head round and straightened her back, smiling but implacable – 'have you made up your minds yet to tell me about Mollie?'

The faces about her changed. There was a moment of sombre, unresponsive silence.

Then Tilly Lewis exclaimed delightedly: 'Why, it's Mrs Jackson! She's been bad with the rheumatics; but got up – and put on her hat for the visitors!'

A withered little woman, a neat black hat perched on her head, walked across the clearing, wearing a dingy black dress and frayed grey cardigan with an air of forlorn propriety.

'Good morning, Myrtle,' Mrs Boyd said. 'I'm sorry to hear you've been having rheumatism.'

'What can you expect, Miss Ann?' The half-caste held herself with some dignity: her faded eyes, ringed like agates, looked up at the pleasantly smiling, healthy, fresh-complex-

160 *dismount* get off a horse
160 *outline* drawing showing essential features but no detail
162 *awe sb.* fill sb. with respect
165 *implacable* unversöhnlich
168 *sombre* ['sɒmbə] dark, dull
168 *unresponsive* not giving a reaction
172 *wither* become smaller due to age or disease
173 *dingy* ['dɪndʒi] dark and dirty
174 *frayed* worn
174 *forlorn* sad and lonely
174 *propriety* [prə'praɪəti] correctness concerning behaviour or morals
179 *agate* ['ægət] hard, coloured stone used in jewellery
180 *fresh-complexioned* good and healthy looking face

Infobox | The Stolen Generations

Mission stations were set up in the outback of Australia to 'civilize' and Christianize Aborigines, who were considered backward and inferior. The main motive was to assimilate Aboriginal children into European society over one or two generations by denying and destroying their Aboriginality. This was done by removing half-caste children from their Aboriginal mother (the father was usually white). Altogether over 100,000 Aboriginal children were taken forcibly from their families by welfare officers. Most were raised in church or state institutions. They received little education, and were expected to go into domestic service or agricultural work. At mission stations it was forbidden for children to speak their own language and practise their ceremonies. Parents were not told where their children were and could not trace them. These children are usually referred to as the 'stolen generation'.

Bobby Randal was taken away from his mother at the age of five by a policeman.

ioned woman on the big horse. 'I'm not used to living out of doors.'

'No, of course not,' Mrs Boyd replied.

'You know I was brought up at the mission station. And I've worked in some of the best homes in the district; but now – you wouldn't keep a sow in the place where I've got to live.'

'It's not right, Mrs Boyd,' George muttered.

'No, it's not right,' Mrs Boyd agreed. 'But what can I do about it? Would you go into the Old Women's Home if I could get you in, Myrtle?'

'I've been there. The police took me from the hospital after I had rheumatic fever. But I ran away –'

'She did, Mrs Boyd!' eager voices chimed.

'She walked near on a hundred and thirty miles till she got here.'

'Cooped up in the city – with a lot of low-down old women treatin' me like dirt. I've always kept myself to myself. I've always been respectable, Miss Ann.'

'Oh, yes, she's terrible respectable, Mrs Boyd,' the chorus went up.

'Nobody can't say Mrs Jackson isn't respectable!'

'All I want's to die in my own place – like any respectable person. It is my own place, Miss Ann, the house your father gave Tom and me; and Mr Henry had no right to turn us out.'

'She's breaking her heart, like any old abo, for the hunting-grounds of her people,' Albert said cynically. 'They always want to go home to die, but, being half-and-half, it's a roof over her head Mrs Jackson wants, and a bed to lie on.'

'I'll see what I can do about it, Myrtle,' Mrs Boyd promised.

'Funny, isn't it?' Albert's lounging, graceful figure tilted back as he gazed at her. 'You're the granddaughter of one of the early settlers who shot off more blacks than any other man in the country. Mrs Jackson is the granddaughter of one of the few survivors, and related to the best families in the district. But you've got the land and the law on your side. They put the dogs onto her if she goes round the homesteads asking for a bit of tucker or old clothes.'

'And this is the only spot where we're allowed to camp in the district.'

'Something will have to be done about it,' Mrs Boyd declared.

'What?' Albert demanded. 'All the land about has been taken up. It's private property now. We're not allowed to work in the mines. We're not allowed to sell the fish we catch

184 *mission station* church mission where half-caste Aboriginal children were taught
186 *sow* adult female pig
194 *chime* join in together
195 *near on* (infml) nearly
197 *cooped up* kept in a small space
197 *low-down* (infml) of bad character
205 *turn sb. out* force sb. to leave a place
209 *half-and-half* half-caste
213 *lounge* stand in a relaxed and lazy way
213 *tilt* kippen, neigen
219 *homestead* farmhouse
220 *tucker* (AustEng infml) food

– not allowed to shoot or trap. They don't want us on the farms. They won't let us work on the roads. All we're allowed to do is draw rations and rot ... though there is some talk of packing us off to one of those damned reservations "where the diseased and dying remnants of the native race are permitted to end their days in peace". Excuse me quoting the local rag.'

'You can't say I haven't tried to help you,' Mrs Boyd protested. 'I've always given you work on my farm when I could.'

A wry smile twisted the young man's mouth. 'And paid us less than half you'd have had to pay other workers.'

'Albert!' one of the women objected. 'Don't take any notice of him, Mrs Boyd.'

'You're talking like one of those crazy agitators, Albert,' Mrs Boyd cried hotly. 'If you're not careful you'll find yourself being moved on.'

'I'll remember you said so, Mrs Boyd.' Albert grinned maliciously.

'It's hard on Albert not being able to get work, Mrs Boyd,' Ruby expostulated. 'He's real clever: can read and write as good as any white man. When he went to school he could beat any of the boys.'

'Lot of good it's ever done me,' Albert sneered. 'If I'd been a myall I'd've had a better life. The blacks of any tribe share all they've got with each other. The whites grab all they can for themselves – and let even their own relations starve.'

'Do the aboriginals treat half-castes better?' Miss Allison's voice rose clear and chilly against his wrath.

'They don't treat us like vermin.' Albert might have been admiring the gleam of her hair or the horse she was holding. 'Up in the nor'-west, when I was a kid, I went around with my mother's tribe. Never knew I was any different from the rest. Then my father got interested in me. Sent me down here to school. He died – and I've been trying to get a job ever since.'

'Do you want to go back to your own people?'

Albert's anger resurged. 'My own people!' he jeered. 'Who are they? My father was as fair as you are. I couldn't live in a blacks' camp now – though this is as bad. But I don't belong there. I think differently. We all do. We like soap and clean clothes when we can get them, and books. We want to go to the pictures and football matches. I want to work and have a house to live in, a wife and kids. But this is all I've got. These are my only people – mongrels like myself.'

'You shouldn't talk bitter like that, Albert,' Mrs Jackson reproved. 'It does no good.'

228 *trap* catch an animal in a trap (= Falle)
230 *draw rations* receive food
230 *rot* verrotten
234 *rag* (infml) low-quality newspaper
237 *wry* [raɪ] using dry humour
241 *agitator* ['ædʒɪteɪtə] person who tries to persuade people to take part in political protest
245 *malicious* showing hatred and the desire to harm sb.
247 *expostulate* argue
251 *myall* ['maɪɔːl] (AustrEng) Aborigine living in the traditional way
253 *starve* suffer or die from hunger
255 *wrath* [rɒθ] extreme anger
256 *vermin* Schädling, Ungeziefer
258 *nor'-west* (dialect) north-west
264 *resurge* come back, become strong again
264 *jeer* speak in a rude way
265 *fair* light-skinned
271 *mongrel* (derog) person of mixed descent
273 *reprove* zurechtweisen

'Nothing does any good.' He flung away from the crowd and stalked off behind the wurlies.

'He's sore because he can't get work and the Protector won't let Penny Carnarvon marry him,' Ruby said. 'Penny's in service, and she's such a good servant they don't want to lose her. But she's fond of Albert. She says she'll learn the Protector.'

'She will, too.'

'Stella did, didn't she?'

'Too right, she did.'

'She dropped a trayload of dishes to get herself the sack because she wanted to marry Bob. But the missus forgave her and took it out of her wages. Stella had to get herself in the family way, and make up to the boss, before the Protector decided she'd better marry Bob.'

'Penny'll be going for a little holiday soon, Albert says. Then perhaps they can get married and go up north. He's almost sure he can get a job on one of the stations.'

'But where's Mollie?' Mrs Boyd returned to the attack. The crowd closed down on their laughter and gossip. There was a disconcerted shuffling and searching for something to say.

'Mollie?'

'Yes, Mollie. It's no use pretending you don't know where she is. If she's hiding, doesn't want to come home, I'm not going to worry about her. But I'll have to let the Department know –'

'Hullo, Mrs Boyd!' A girl in a pink cotton frock stood in the opening of a wurley behind the horses. A pretty little thing, sturdy and self-possessed, but rather pale, she stood there, a small bundle wrapped in a dirty shawl in her arms.

'Mollie,' Mrs Boyd gasped. 'Have you been getting a baby?'

The girl nodded, smiling.

'But you're only a child,' Mrs Boyd cried. 'You're not sixteen.'

'I was sixteen last month,' Mollie replied calmly.

'It's scandalous,' Mrs Boyd exclaimed indignantly. 'Who's the father?'

Mollie's eyes smiled back at her. 'I been going with two or three boys in town.'

The little crowd before her quivered to breathless excitement: a sigh, as of relief, and a titter of suppressed mirth escaped.

'You ought to be ashamed of yourself,' Mrs Boyd declared furiously. 'You know, I thought better of you, Mollie. I thought you were different from the other girls. You've lived

274 *fling away* (here) go quickly and angrily
275 *stalk off* walk in a proud or angry manner
276 *sore* (infml) angry
276 *Protector* government official responsible for protecting the rights of Aboriginal Australians and controlling their lives
277 *be in service* work as a servant
279 *learn sb.* change sb.'s opinion
284 *get the sack* be fired
285 *missus* lady of the house
286 *in the family way* (infml) pregnant
287 *make up to sb.* be on good terms with sb.
294 *disconcerted* confused, embarrassed
294 *shuffle* move from one foot to another
299 *Department* Department of Aboriginal Affairs
301 *frock* dress
303 *sturdy* confident
303 *self-possessed* in control of your feelings
304 *shawl* large piece of cloth used to keep the shoulders warm
305 *gasp* take a quick deep breath due to surprise
311 *indignant* feeling or showing annoyance
315 *quiver* shake, tremble
316 *titter* short laugh
316 *mirth* amusement

with me for so many years, and I trusted you to behave yourself.'

'Don't be angry,' Mollie said quietly. 'I couldn't help it ... and I like the baby.'

'When did it happen?'

'Last night.'

Mrs Boyd stared at the girl. She looked a little wan, but quite well.

'Is she all right?' she asked the crone who had come out of the hut behind Mollie. 'Had I better get the doctor to come out and see her, or arrange for her to go into hospital?'

'I've never felt better in my life,' Mollie said. 'Aunty May can look after me.'

'No need to bother,' the old half-caste beside Mollie mumbled soothingly. 'She hadn't a bad time. I'd have sent her to the hospital – but everything happened in such a hurry.'

'Let me see the child,' Mrs Boyd demanded: turned her horse and rode to Mollie.

'She's very little and red,' Mollie apologized, tenderly lifting the dirty shawl that covered the baby.

Mrs Boyd leaned down from her saddle. It was the ugliest scrap of humanity she had ever seen; but there was something vaguely familiar in its tiny crumpled face. Cecily Allison dragged her horse over the grass to look at the baby, too.

'Ra-ther sweet, isn't she?' she murmured mechanically. 'What are you going to call her?'

Mollie drew the shawl over the baby's face again.

'Marlene,' she said happily.

The rain descended in a gusty squall, driving the half-castes into their wurlies, the horsewomen back among the trees. As they rode, the older woman sagged in her saddle, curiously aged and grim.

'The sooner they're cleaned out of the district the better,' she said viciously. 'They're an immoral lot, these half-castes.'

'What about the whites who are responsible for them?' the girl on the chestnut colt asked.

She wondered whether it was a tragedy or a comedy she had been witnessing. These people might live like dogs in their rotten wurlies, with the dark bush behind them and the prosperous little township spread at their feet; but their aspirations were all towards the ways and ideas of the white race. The exotic film-star, and that baby in this dump of outcasts – what an indictment! ~~Yet Miss Allison suspected~~ Yet Miss Allison suspected they had tried to spare the baby's grand-

One of the many Aborigine girls who was taken from her family and made to work as a servant

327 *wan* [wɒn] pale, appearing ill
329 *crone* ugly old woman
336 *soothing* gentle, calm
344 *scrap* small piece or amount of sth.
351 *descend* come down
351 *squall* sudden gust of wind
353 *sag* sink downwards
354 *curiously* strangely, unusually
356 *vicious* cruel, nasty
356 *lot* (infml) group
362 *prosperous* successful or flourishing
362 *aspiration* hope, ambition
364 *film-star* reference to Marlene Dietrich (1901–1992), German-born actress
364 *outcast* person who is not accepted by other people
365 *indictment* [ɪn'daɪtmənt] sign that a society is bad or wrong
366 *spare sb* prevent sb. from going through an unpleasant experience

mother, with simple kindliness, knowing the truth behind Mollie's bravado. Had they altogether succeeded?

The camp on the hillside was moved on before the end of the month.

368 *bravado* way of behaving that is intended to impress people

Tasks

1 Describe the living conditions of the half-castes as depicted in the short story.

2 Explain the problems the half-castes experience in dealing with their identity.

3 Examine the depiction of white people in the story.

4 Explain the last sentence of the story.

5 Predict how the life of Molly's baby is going to develop.

Additional Text:
Kevin Rudd Apology to Australia's Indiginous People

Om 12 February 2008, Prime Minister Kevin Rudd gave a speech many had been waiting for: he said sorry to the 'stolen generations'.

I move:

That today we honour the indigenous peoples of this land, the oldest continuing cultures in human history.

We reflect on their past mistreatment.

We reflect in particular on the mistreatment of those who were stolen generations – this blemished chapter in our nation's history.

The time has now come for the nation to turn a new page in Australia's history by righting the wrongs of the past and so moving forward with confidence to the future.

We apologise for the laws and policies of successive parliaments and governments that have inflicted profound grief, suffering and loss on these our fellow Australians.

We apologise especially for the removal of Aboriginal and Torres Strait Islander children from their families, their communities and their country.

For the pain, suffering and hurt of these stolen generations, their descendants and for their families left behind, we say sorry.

To the mothers and the fathers, the brothers and the sisters, for the breaking up of families and communities, we say sorry.

And for the indignity and degradation thus inflicted on a proud people and a proud culture, we say sorry.

We the Parliament of Australia respectfully request that this apology be received in the spirit in which it is offered as part of the healing of the nation.

For the future we take heart; resolving that this new page in the history of our great continent can now be written.

We today take this first step by acknowledging the past and laying claim to a future that embraces all Australians.

A future where this parliament resolves that the injustices of the past must never, never happen again.

A future where we harness the determination of all Australians, indigenous and non-indigenous, to close the gap that lies between us in life expectancy, educational achievement and economic opportunity.

A future where we embrace the possibility of new solutions to enduring problems where old approaches have failed.

A future based on mutual respect, mutual resolve and mutual responsibility.

1 *move* put forward a motion (= Antrag) in parliament
6 *blemished* spoiled
12 *inflict sth. on sb.* make sb. suffer sth.
15 *Torres Strait Islander* Aborigine living on a group of islands off the north coast of Australia
21 *indignity* Demütigung
21 *degradation* Erniedrigung
26 *resolve* make a firm decision
28 *acknowledge sth.* accept that sth. is true
28 *lay claim to sth.* say that sth. belongs to you
29 *embrace sth.* (fml) include sth.
32 *harness sth.* control and use the strength of sth.
36 *embrace sth.* accept sth. with enthusiasm
37 *enduring* lasting a long time
37 *approach* way of dealing with sth.
38 *mutual* gegenseitig
38 *resolve* (n) strong determinaiton

A future where all Australians, whatever their origins, are truly equal partners, with equal opportunities and with an equal stake in shaping the next chapter in the history of this great country, Australia.

There comes a time in the history of nations when their peoples must become fully reconciled to their past if they are to go forward with confidence to embrace their future.

Our nation, Australia, has reached such a time.

That is why the Parliament is today here assembled: to deal with this unfinished business of the nation, to remove a great stain from the nation's soul and, in a true spirit of reconciliation, to open a new chapter in the history of this great land, Australia. [...]

Some have asked, Why apologise?

Let me begin to answer by telling the Parliament just a little of one person's story – an elegant, eloquent and wonderful woman in her 80s, full of life, full of funny stories, despite what has happened in her life's journey, a woman who has travelled a long way to be with us today, a member of the stolen generation who shared some of her story with me when I called around to see her just a few days ago. Nanna Nungala Fejo, as she prefers to be called, was born in the late 1920s. She remembers her earliest childhood days living with her family and her community in a bush camp just outside Tennant Creek. She remembers the love and the warmth and the kinship of those days long ago, including traditional dancing around the camp fire at night. She loved the dancing. She remembers once getting into strife when, as a four-year-old girl, she insisted on dancing with the male tribal elders rather than just sitting and watching the men, as the girls were supposed to do.

But then, sometime around 1932, when she was about four, she remembers the coming of the welfare men. Her family had feared that day and had dug holes in the creek bank where the children could run and hide. What they had not expected was that the white welfare men did not come alone. They brought a truck, two white men and an Aboriginal stockman on horseback cracking his stockwhip. The kids were found; they ran for their mothers, screaming, but they could not get away. They were herded and piled onto the back of the truck. Tears flowing, her mum tried clinging to the sides of the truck as her children were taken away to the Bungalow in Alice, all in the name of protection.

A few years later, government policy changed. Now the children would be handed over to the missions to be cared for by the churches. But which church would care for them? The kids were

41 *stake* Anteil
45 *become reconciled to sth.* accept sth. that you find unpleasant
50 *stain* mark that is difficult to remove
50 *reconciliation* Versöhnung
63 *Tennant Creek* small town in the Northern Territory
66 *strife* angry conflict
72 *creek* (AustrEng) small river
75 *stockman* (AustrEng) man who looks after cattle on a large property
75 *crack sth.* make a sharp sound with sth.
76 *stockwhip* (AustrEng) whip used to drive cattle
77 *herd sb./sth.* force sb./sth. to move together like animals
79 *cling to sth.* hold tightly onto sth.
80 *the Bungalow* institution in which Aborigine children were kept
80 *Alice* Alice Springs

simply told to line up in three lines. Nanna Fejo and her sister stood in the middle line, her older brother and cousin on her left. Those on the left were told that they had become Catholics, those in the middle Methodists and those on the right Church of England. That is how the complex questions of post-reformation theology were resolved in the Australian outback in the 1930s. It was as crude as that. She and her sister were sent to a Methodist mission on Goulburn Island and then Croker Island. Her Catholic brother was sent to work at a cattle station and her cousin to a Catholic mission. Nanna Fejo's family had been broken up for a second time. She stayed at the mission until after the war, when she was allowed to leave for a prearranged job as a domestic in Darwin. She was 16. Nanna Fejo never saw her mum again. After she left the mission, her brother let her know that her mum had died years before, a broken woman fretting for the children that had literally been ripped away from her.

I asked Nanna Fejo what she would have me say today about her story. She thought for a few moments then said that what I should say today was that 'all mothers are important'. And she added: 'Families – keeping them together is very important. It's a good thing that you are surrounded by love and that love is passed down the generations. That's what gives you happiness.' [...]

Nanna Fejo's is just one story. There are thousands, tens of thousands of them: stories of forced separation of Aboriginal and Torres Strait Islander children from their mums and dads over the better part of a century. [...]

These stories cry out to be heard; they cry out for an apology.

Instead, from the nation's Parliament there has been a stony, stubborn and deafening silence for more than a decade; a view that somehow we, the Parliament, should suspend our most basic instincts of what is right and what is wrong; a view that, instead, we should look for any pretext to push this great wrong to one side, to leave it languishing with the historians, the academics and the cultural warriors, as if the stolen generations are little more than an interesting sociological phenomenon.

But the stolen generations are not intellectual curiosities. They are human beings, human beings who have been damaged deeply by the decisions of parliaments and governments. But, as of today, the time for denial, the time for delay, has at last come to an end. The nation is demanding of its political leadership to take us forward. Decency, human decency, universal human decency, demands that the nation now step forward to right an historical wrong. That is what we are doing in this place today.

But should there still be doubts as to why we must now act, let the Parliament reflect for a moment on the following facts: that,

90 *crude* done in a way which is simple and primitive
91 *Goulburn Island, Croker Island* islands off the northern coast of Australia
95 *domestic* person working as a servant in a sb.'s private home
96 *Darwin* city in the north of Australia
98 *fret for sb.* be worried about sb. so that you cannot relax
99 *literally* buchstäblich
99 *rip sb./sth. away* take sb./sth. away by force
116 *languish* stay somewhere unpleasant for a long time
117 *cultural warrior* people who are interested in examining cultural awareness
122 *denial* [dəˈnaɪəl] Leugnen
125 *right a wrong* ein Unrecht wieder gutmachen

between 1910 and 1970, between 10 and 30% of indigenous children were forcibly taken from their mothers and fathers; that, as a result, up to 50,000 children were forcibly taken from their families; that this was the product of the deliberate, calculated policies of the state as reflected in the explicit powers given to them under statute; that this policy was taken to such extremes by some in administrative authority that the forced extractions of children of so-called mixed lineage were seen as part of a broader policy of dealing with the problem of the Aboriginal population.

One of the most notorious examples of this approach was from the Northern Territory Protector of Natives, who stated: 'Generally by the fifth and invariably by the sixth generation, all native characteristics of the Australian Aborigine are eradicated. The problem of our half-castes' – to quote the protector – 'will quickly be eliminated by the complete disappearance of the black race, and the swift submergence of their progeny in the white'. [...]

These are uncomfortable things to be brought out into the light. They are not pleasant. They are profoundly disturbing. But we must acknowledge these facts if we are to deal once and for all with the argument that the policy of generic forced separation was somehow well motivated, justified by its historical context and, as a result, unworthy of any apology today. [...]

As has been said of settler societies elsewhere, we are the bearers of many blessings from our ancestors; therefore we must also be the bearer of their burdens as well. Therefore, for our nation, the course of action is clear: that is, to deal now with what has become one of the darkest chapters in Australia's history.

In doing so, we are doing more than contending with the facts, the evidence and the often rancorous public debate. In doing so, we are also wrestling with our own soul. This is not, as some would argue, a black-armband view of history; it is just the truth: the cold, confronting, uncomfortable truth – facing it, dealing with it, moving on from it. Until we fully confront that truth, there will always be a shadow hanging over us and our future as a fully united and fully reconciled people.

It is time to reconcile. It is time to recognise the injustices of the past. It is time to say sorry. It is time to move forward together.

To the stolen generations, I say the following: as Prime Minister of Australia, I am sorry.

On behalf of the Government of Australia, I am sorry.

On behalf of the Parliament of Australia, I am sorry.

I offer you this apology without qualification.

We apologise for the hurt, the pain and suffering that we, the

132 *deliberate* done on purpose
133 *explicit* that was clearly expressed
134 *statute* law passed by parliament
135 *extraction* removal
136 *lineage* ['lɪniɪdʒ] race or family from which a person comes from
138 *notorious* famous for being bad
139 *Protector of the Natives* government official responsible for protecting the rights of Aboriginal Australians and controlling their lives
141 *eradicate sth.* get rid of sth. completely
144 *submergence* disappearance of sth. into sth. else
144 *progeny* ['prɒdʒəni] children
149 *generic* general
152 *bearer* carrier
158 *rancorous* noisy and bitter
160 *black-armband* (here) very negative
164 *reconcile (sb./sth. with sb./sth.)* ['rekənsaɪl] (jdn./etwas mit jdm./etwas) versöhnen

parliament, have caused you by the laws that previous parliaments have enacted.

We apologise for the indignity, the degradation and the humiliation these laws embodied.

We offer this apology to the mothers, the fathers, the brothers, the sisters, the families and the communities whose lives were ripped apart by the actions of successive governments under successive parliaments.

In making this apology, I would also like to speak personally to the members of the stolen generations and their families: to those here today, so many of you; to those listening across the nation.

From: *'Text of PM Rudd's "sorry" address',* The Age, *13 February 2008*

Tasks

1. Describe your reaction to the speech by Prime Minister Rudd.
2. Explain how the information from this speech affects your attitude to the short story 'Marlene' by Prichard.
3. Find examples of repetition, enumeration as well as parallel sentence structures in the prime minister's speech and analyse their function.

ARCHIE WELLER **Going Home**

Archie Weller (born 1957) is an Australian novelist and writer of short stories and screenplays. Weller was born in Cranbrook, Western Australia, and was brought up on a remote farm before being sent to boarding school in Perth. He interrupted his degree at the Western Australian Institute of Technology to work on his first novel *The Day of the Dog* (1981), in which he portrays poverty and violence in contemporary Australia. In his short story collection *Going Home* (1986), from which this story is taken, he examines Aboriginal identity. Weller also wrote the screenplay for the film *First Citizen* (1988) about the Aboriginal artist Albert Manatjira.

In 'Going Home' Weller shows the problems of a young Aboriginal man who is uncertain about his own identity as a black man trying to follow the lifestyle of white people.

I want to go home.
I want to go home.
Oh, Lord, I want to go home.

Charlie Pride moans from a cassette, and his voice slips out of the crack the window makes. Out into the world of magpies' soothing carols, and parrots' cheeky whistles, of descending darkness and spirits.

The man doesn't know that world. His is the world of the sleek new Kingswood that speeds down the never-ending highway.

At last he can walk this earth with pride, as his ancestors did many years before him. He had his first exhibition of paintings a month ago. They sold well, and with the proceeds he bought the car.

The slender black hands swing the shiny black wheel around a corner. Blackness forms a unison of power.

For five years he has worked hard and saved and sacrificed. Now, on his twenty-first birthday, he is going home.

New car, new clothes, new life.

He plucks a cigarette from the packet beside him, and lights up.

His movements are elegant and delicate. His hair is well-groomed, and his clothes are clean.

Billy Woodward is coming home in all his might, in his shining armour.

*

4 *Charlie Pride* (born 1938) black American country singer
4 *moan* express a sound of suffering
5 *magpie* Elster
6 *soothing* gentle, calm
6 *carol* type of song (usu. associated with Christmas)
6 *descend* move downwards
9 *sleek* expensive and elegant
9 *Kingswood* type of car
13 *proceeds* (pl) money an artist gets from the sale of his or her works
16 *unison* (here) unity
23 *well-groomed* neatly combed
25 *armour* protective covering made of steel, worn by medieval knights

Sixteen years old. Last year at school.

His little brother Carlton and his cousin Rennie Davis, down beside the river, on that last night before he went to the college in Perth, when all three had had a goodbye drink, with their girls beside them.

Frogs croaking into the silent hot air and some animal blundering in the bulrushes on the other side of the gentle river. Moonlight on the ruffled water. Nasal voices whispering and giggling. The clink of beer bottles.

That year at college, with all its schoolwork, and learning, and discipline, and uniformity, he stood out alone in the football carnival.

Black hands grab the ball. Black feet kick the ball. Black hopes go soaring with the ball to the pasty white sky.

No one can stop him now. He forgets about the river of his Dreaming and the people of his blood and the girl in his heart.

The year when he was eighteen, he was picked by a top city team as a rover. This was the year that he played for the state, where he was voted best and fairest on the field.

That was a year to remember.

He never went out to the park at Guildford, so he never saw his people: his dark, silent staring people, his rowdy, brawling, drunk people.

He was white now.

Once, in the middle of the night, one of his uncles had crept around to the house he rented and fallen asleep on the verandah. A dirty pitiful carcass, encased in the black greatcoat that had smelt of stale drink and lonely, violent places. A withered black hand had clutched an almost empty metho bottle.

In the morning, Billy had shouted at the old man and pushed him down the steps, where he stumbled and fell without pride. The old man had limped out of the creaking gate, not understanding.

The white neighbours, wakened by the noise, had peered out of their windows at the staggering old man stumbling down the street and the glowering youth muttering on the verandah. They had smirked in self-righteous knowledge.

Billy had moved on the next day.

William Jacob Woodward passed fifth year with flying colours. All the teachers were proud of him. He went to the West Australian Institute of Technology to further his painting, to gain fame that way as well.

He bought clean, bright clothes and cut off his long hair that all the camp girls had loved.

32 *blunder* move in a clumsy way
32 *bulrush* marsh or water plant
33 *ruffle sth.* disturb sth. (e.g. a quiet surface)
33 *nasal* sounding as if it is coming through the nose
37 *football* (here) Australian Rules football, a sport invented in Australia
37 *carnival* (here) everything that is connected with a particular thing
39 *soar* fly high
39 *pasty* ['peɪsti] pale
41 *Dreaming* belief of the Aborigines that every person has a special relationship with certain plants, animals, places or other features in nature, by which he or she is connected to a spiritual reality called 'Dreamtime'
44 *rover* position in an Australian Rules football team
47 *the park* (here) area on the edge of a town where Aborigines live
48 *rowdy* noisy, getting into arguments
49 *brawl* fight
53 *carcass* (here) person looking like a dead body
53 *encase sth.* surround sth., enclose sth.
55 *withered* thin and weak due to age, etc.
55 *metho* (infml) = *methylated spirits* cheap type of alcohol
59 *limp* walk with difficulty
63 *glower* ['glaʊə] stare
63 *mutter* talk quietly so it is difficult for others to understand you
64 *smirk* smile in way that shows you feel pleased with yourself
67 *with flying colours* with excellent marks
72 *camp* (here) living on campus

Billy Woodward was a handsome youth, with the features of his white grandfather and the quietness of his Aboriginal forebears. He stood tall and proud, with the sensitive lips of a dreamer and a faraway look in his serene amber eyes.

He went to the nightclubs regularly and lost his soul in the throbbing, writhing electrical music as the white tribe danced their corroboree to the good life.

He would sit along at the darkened corner table, or with a painted-up white girl – but mostly alone. He would drink wine and look around the room at all the happy or desperate people.

He was walking home one night from a nightclub when a middle-aged Aboriginal woman stumbled out of a lane.

She grinned up at him like the Gorgon and her hands clutched at his body, like the lights from the nightclub.

75 *forebear* ancestor
76 *serene* calm, peaceful
76 *amber* Bernstein
79 *writhe* [raɪð] twist or roll about painfully
80 *corroboree* [kəˈrɒbəri] traditional Aboriginal gathering, often accompanied by dances and songs
87 *Gorgon* (in Greek mythology) one of three winged monstrous sisters

Infobox | Aboriginal art

Aborigines had for centuries created rock carvings and sculptures, most of which had a spiritual meaning. Following the arrival of the Europeans, Aborigines spent nearly two centuries trying to fight for their existence. In 1934 Australian painter Rex Batterbee taught Aboriginal artists Western style watercolour landscape painting. These paintings became popular and sold out when the paintings were exhibited.

From the 1960s onwards people became more interested in traditional themes in Aboriginal art. In 1966, the Australian one dollar note used a design by an Aboriginal artist. In the 1970s Aboriginal artists started to use 'dot paintings' to put their stories onto canvas. These stories had previously been drawn on the desert sand, and were now given a more permanent form. What is seen today as Aboriginal art is largely derived from this movement. Aboriginal art has become a big business worldwide.

The painting here depicts the Rainbow Snake, a personification of fertility and rain. The snake is a creator of human beings, having life-giving powers. It is also responsible for storms and floods when it acts as an agent of punishment against those who break the law. Rainbow snakes can also enter a man and endow him with magical powers, or leave 'little rainbows' within his body which will make him ill and die. It is worth considering this information when thinking about the snake in the short story 'The Drover's Wife'.

'Billy! Ya Billy Woodward, unna?'

'Yes. What of it?' he snapped.

'Ya dunno me? I'm ya Aunty Rose, from down Koodup.'

She cackled then. Ugly, oh, so ugly. Yellow and red eyes and broken teeth and a long, crooked, white scar across her temple. Dirty grey hair all awry.

His people.

His eyes clouded over in revulsion. He shoved her away and walked off quickly.

He remembered her face for many days afterwards whenever he tried to paint a picture. He felt ashamed to be related to a thing like that. He was bitter that she was of his blood.

That was his life: painting pictures and playing football and pretending. But his people knew. They always knew.

In his latest game of football he had a young part-Aboriginal opponent who stared at him the whole game with large, scornful black eyes seeing right through him.

After the game, the boy's family picked him up in an old battered station wagon.

Billy, surrounded by all his white friends, saw them from afar off. He saw the children kicking an old football about with yells and shouts of laughter and two lanky boys slumping against the door yarning to their hero, and a buxom girl leaning out the window and an old couple in the back. The three boys, glancing up, spotted debonair Billy. Their smiles faded for an instant and they speared him with their proud black eyes.

So Billy was going home, because he had been reminded of home (with all its carefree joys) at that last match.

It's raining now. The shafts slant down from the sky, in the glare of the headlights. Night-time, when woodarchis come out to kill, leaving no tracks: as though they are cloud shadows passing over the sun.

Grotesque trees twist in the half-light. Black tortured figures, with shaggy heads and pleading arms. Ancestors crying for remembrance. Voices shriek or whisper in tired chants: tired from the countless warnings that have not been heeded.

They twirl around the man, like the lights of the city he knows. But he cannot understand these trees. They drag him onwards, even when he thinks of turning back and not going on to where he vowed he would never go again.

A shape, immovable and impressive as the tree it is under, steps into the road on the Koodup turnoff.

An Aboriginal man.

Billy slews to a halt, or he will run the man over.

89 *ya* (sl) you
89 *unna* (sl) aren't you
91 *dunno* (infml) don't know
92 *cackle* laugh in a loud, harsh way
94 *awry* [ə'raɪ] in disorder
96 *revulsion* sense of disgust and loathing
96 *shove sb./sth.* away push sb./sth. away
108 *station wagon* Kombi(wagen)
111 *lanky* lean, with thin legs
112 *slump against sth.* lean against sth.
112 *yarn* (infml) talk in a jokey way
113 *buxom* plump, round
114 *debonair* [ˌdebə'neə] fashionable and confident
119 *slant down* fall at an angle
120 *woodarchi* evil spirit
124 *shaggy* with rough, disorderly hair
126 *chant* rhythmic phrase that is repeated continually (esp. in religious services)
127 *heed sth.* pay attention to sth., take notice of sth.
133 *turnoff* road leading off a main road
135 *slew* (here) stop the car quickly so it slides in another direction

Door opens.

Wind and rain and coloured man get in.

'Ta, mate. It's bloody cold 'ere,' the coloured man grates, then stares quizzically at Billy, with sharp black eyes. 'Nyoongah, are ya, mate?'

'Yes.'

The man sniffs noisily, and rubs a sleeve across his nose.

'Well, I'm Darcy Goodrich, at any rate, bud.'

He holds out a calloused hand. Yellow-brown, blunt scarred fingers, dirty nails. A lifetime of sorrow is held between the fingers.

Billy takes it limply.

'I'm William Woodward.'

'Yeah?' Fathomless eyes scrutinise him again from behind the scraggly black hair that falls over his face.

'Ya goin' anywheres near Koodup, William?'

'Yes.'

'Goodoh. This is a nice car ya got 'ere. Ya must 'ave plen'y of boya, unna?'

Silence from Billy.

He would rather not have this cold, wet man beside him, reminding him.

He keeps his amber eyes on the lines of the road as they flash under his wheels.

White ... white ... white ...

'Ya got a smoke, William?'

'Certainly. Help yourself.'

Black blunt fingers flick open his expensive cigarette case.

'Ya want one too, koordah?'

'Thanks.'

'Ya wouldn't be Teddy Woodward's boy, would ya, William?'

'Yes, that's right. How are Mum and Dad – and everyone?'

Suddenly he has to know all about his family and becomes lost in their sea of brownness.

Darcy's craggy face flickers at him in surprise, then turns, impassive again, to the rain-streaked window. He puffs on his cigarette quietly.

'What, ya don't know?' he says softly. 'Ya Dad was drinkin' metho. 'E was blind drunk, an' in the 'orrors, ya know? Well, this truck came out of nowhere when 'e was crossin' the road on a night like this. Never seen 'im. Never stopped or nothing'. Ya brother Carl found 'im next day an'

138 *ta* (sl) thank you
138 *grate* speak in a harsh tone
139 *quizzical* curious
139 *Nyoongah* name by which the Aborigines of the south-west of Western Australia refer to themselves
144 *bud* (sl) = *buddy* (infml) mate, friend
145 *calloused* hard and leathery
145 *blunt* not sharp or round-shaped
146 *scarred* narbig
150 *fathomless* having no end or bottom
150 *scrutinise sb./sth.* watch, observe sb./sth. closely
151 *scraggly* thin and gowing in a way that is not tidy
154 *goodoh* (infml) great
155 *plen'y* (dialect) plenty
155 *boya* (Aboriginal language) money
166 *koordah* (Aboriginal language) brother, friend
174 *craggy* (here) rough, with many wrinkles
178 *the 'orrors* = *the horrors* „Säuferwahnsinn", Delirium tremens

there was nothin' no one could do then. That was a couple of years back now.'

Billy would have been nineteen then, at the peak of his football triumph. On one of those bright white nights, when he had celebrated his victories with wine and white women, Billy's father had been wiped off the face of his country – all alone.

He can remember his father as a small gentle man who was the best card cheat in the camp. He could make boats out of duck feathers and he and Carlton and Billy had had races by the muddy side of the waterhole, from where his people had come long ago, in the time of the beginning.

The lights of Koodup grin at him as he swings around a bend. Pinpricks of eyes, like a pack of foxes waiting for the blundering black rabbit. 'Tell ya what, buddy. Stop off at the hotel an' buy a carton of stubbies.'

'All right, Darcy.' Billy smiles and looks closely at the man for the first time. He desperately feels that he needs a friend as he goes back into the open mouth of his previous life. Darcy gives a gap-toothed grin.

'Bet ya can't wait to see ya people again.'

His people: ugly Aunty Rose, the metho-drinking Uncle, his dead forgotten father, his wild brother and cousin. Even this silent man. They are all his people.

He can never escape.

The car creeps in beside the red brick hotel.

The two Nyoongahs scurry through the rain and shadows and into the glare of the small hotel bar.

The barman is a long time coming, although the bar is almost empty. Just a few old cockies and young larrikins, right down the other end. Arrogant grey eyes stare at Billy. No feeling there at all.

'A carton of stubbies, please.'

'Only if you bastards drink it down at the camp. Constable told me you mob are drinking in town and just causing trouble.'

'We'll drink where we bloody like, thanks, mate.'

'Will you, you cheeky bastard?' The barman looks at Billy, in surprise. 'Well then, you're not gettin' nothin' from me.

You can piss off, too, before I call the cops. They'll cool you down, you smart black bastard.'

Something hits Billy deep inside with such a force that it makes him want to clutch hold of the bar and spew up all his pride.

He is black and the barman is white, and nothing can ever change that.

195 *pinpricks of eyes* (here) narrow eyes that are watching carefully
196 *blunder* make a stupid mistake
197 *stubby* (AustEng sl): small bottle of beer
208 *scurry* walk or run with quick steps
211 *cocky* (AustEng) small farmer
211 *larrikin* (AustEng) young man who likes to make noise
219 *cheeky* frech
225 *spew up* throw up, vomit

All the time he had gulped in the wine and joy of the nightclubs and worn neat fashionable clothes and had white women admiring him, played the white man's game with more skill than most of the wadgulas and painted his country in white man colours to be gabbled over by the wadgulas: all this time he has ignored his mumbling, stumbling tribe and thought he was someone better.

Yet when it comes down to it all, he is just a black man.

Darcy sidles up to the fuming barman.

''Scuse me, Mr 'Owett, but William 'ere just come 'ome, see,' he whines like a beaten dog. 'We will be drinkin' in the camp, ya know.'

'Just come home, eh? What was he inside for?'

Billy bites his reply back so it stays in his stomach, hard and hurtful as a gallstone.

'Well all right, Darcy. I'll forget about it this time. Just keep your friend out of my hair.'

Good dog, Darcy. Have a bone, Darcy. Or will a carton of stubbies do?

Out into the rain again.

They drive away and then turn down a track about a kilometre out of town.

Darcy tears off a bottle top, handing the bottle to Billy. He grins.

'Act stupid, buddy, an' ya go a lo–ong way in this town.'

Billy takes a long draught of the bitter gold liquid. It pours down his throat and into his mind like a shaft of amber sunlight after a gale. He lets his anger subside.

'What ya reckon, Darcy? I'm twenty-one today.'

Darcy thrusts out a hand, beaming.

'Tw'n'y-bloody-one, eh? 'Ow's it feel?'

'No different from yesterday.'

Billy clasps the offered hand firmly.

They laugh and clink bottles together in a toast, just as they reach the camp.

Dark and wet, with a howling wind. Rain beating upon the shapeless humpies. Trees thrash around the circle of the clearing in a violent rhythm of sorrow and anger, like great monsters dancing around a carcass.

Darcy indicates a hut clinging to the edge of the clearing.

'That's where ya mum lives.'

A rickety shape of nailed-down tin and sheets of iron. Two oatbags, sewn together, form a door. Floundering in a sea of tins and rags and parts of toys or cars. Mud everywhere.

232 *wadgula* (Aboriginal language) white people
233 *gabble* talk rapidly and meaninglessly
237 *sidle* ['saɪdl] move in an uncertain way
237 *fuming* (infml) very angry
241 *inside* (infml) in prison
256 *gale* very strong wind
256 *subside* become less intense
257 *reckon* (infml) think
265 *humpy* (AustEng) crude Aborigine hut or shelter, esp. a shanty built at the edge of a town
265 *thrash* move violently
266 *clearing* (n) open space
271 *rickety* badly built, insecure
272 *oatbag* Hafersack
272 *flounder* (here) be unmoveable in the middle of sth. unpleasant

Infobox | Aborigines

It is believed that the Aborigines arrived in Australia approximately 45,000 years ago. At this time, the indigenous Australians lived as semi-nomads and as hunter-gatherers with a strong dependence on the land for survival. Following the arrival of Europeans in the 18th and 19th centuries, Aborigines died in large numbers due to the arrival of new illnesses and diseases. Moreover, they were displaced from their lands and often killed in skirmishes as they tried to defend their land. The settlers believed that because the Aborigines were nomads, they had no concept of land ownership, and could therefore be driven off land needed for farming. However, the loss of traditional lands, food sources and water resources led not only to starvation but also to the destruction of their spiritual life. Aborigines had a deep spiritual and cultural connection to the land, so that when they were forced to move away from traditional areas, cultural and spiritual practices necessary to the cohesion and well-being of the group could not be maintained. Proximity to settlers also resulted in alcohol and substance abuse, due to the loss of their old social and religious structures. Alcohol and drug abuse have remained chronic problems for Aborigines ever since.

It is estimated that between 1788 and 1900 the number of Aborigines decreased by about 90%. Entire communities in the fertile southern part of the continent disappeared before their existence was even properly recorded. Aborigines were consigned to history, and found themselves living in appalling conditions. Since the 1960s, reconciliation has been the main theme behind European and Aborigine Australian relations. Aborigines were finally given the right to vote in elections in 1963. In the 1970s courts began to recognize that the Aborigines did indeed have land claims. In 2010 there were an estimated 500,000 Aborigines in Australia making up 2.5% of the total population. The largest number of Aborigines lives in New South Wales, but in Northern Territory Aborigines make up the largest percentage of the population (ca. 32.5%). Despite the attempt to improve Aborigine living conditions, the majority still live unemployed in temporary camps outside cities and towns. While white male Australians have one of the highest life expectancies in the world (78.7 years), male Aborigines have a life expectancy of just 67 years.

Billy pulls up as close to the door as he can get. He had forgotten what his house really looked like.

'Come on, koordah. Come an' see ya ole mum. Ya might be lucky, too, an' catch ya brother.'

Billy can't say anything. He gets slowly out of the car while the dereliction looms up around him.

The rain pricks at him, feeling him over.

He is one of the brotherhood.

A mouth organ's reedy notes slip in and out between the rain. It is at once a profoundly sorrowful yet carefree tune that goes on and on.

Billy's fanfare home.

He follows Darcy, ducking under the bag door. He feels unsure and out of place and terribly alone.

There are six people: two old women, an ancient man, two youths and a young, shy, pregnant woman.

The youth nearest the door glances up with a black yellowish face, suspicion embedded deep in his black eyes. His long black hair that falls over his shoulders in gentle curls is kept from his face by a red calico headband. Red for the desert sands whence his ancestors came, red for the blood spilt by his ancestors when the white tribe came. Red, the only bright thing in these drab surroundings.

The youth gives a faint smile at Darcy and the beer.

'G'day, Darcy. Siddown 'ere. 'Oo ya mate is?'

'Oo'd ya think, Carl, ya dopy prick? 'E's ya brother come 'ome.'

Carlton stares at Billy incredulously, then his smile widens a little and he stands up, extending a slim hand.

They shake hands and stare deep into each other's faces, smiling. Brown-black and brown-yellow. They let their happiness soak silently into each other.

Then his cousin Rennie, also tall and slender like a young boomer, with bushy red-tinged hair and eager grey eyes, shakes hands. He introduces Billy to his young woman, Phyllis, and reminds him who old China Groves and Florrie-Waters (his mother's parents) are.

His mother sits silently at the scarred kitchen table. Her wrinkled brown face has been battered around, and one of her eyes is sightless. The other stares at his son with a bleak pride of her own.

From that womb I came, Billy thinks, like a flower from the ground or a fledgling from a nest. From out of the reserve I flew.

Where is beauty now?

He remembers his mother as a laughing brown woman, with long black hair in plaits, singing soft songs as she

277 *ole* (dialect) old
280 *dereliction* neglect, decay
283 *reedy* having a thin sound
293 *curl* Locke
294 *calico* type of cloth
299 *g'day* Australian greeting
299 *siddown* (dialect) sit down
299 *'Oo ya mate is?* (dialect) Who is your mate?
300 *dopy prick* (sl) idiot
302 *incredulous* unwilling or unable to believe sth.
308 *boomer* (AustEng) large male kangaroo
316 *womb* [wu:m] (Mutter)schoß
317 *fledgling* baby bird
320 *plaits* [plæts] (pl) Zöpfe

cleaned the house or cooked food. Now she is old and stupid in the mourning of her man.

'So ya came back after all. Ya couldn't come back for ya Dad's funeral, but – unna? Ya too good for us mob, I s'pose,' she whispers in a thin voice like the mouth organ before he even says hello, then turns her eyes back into her pain.

'It's my birthday, Mum. I wanted to see everybody. No one told me Dad was dead.'

Carlton looks up at Billy.

'I make out ya twenty-one, Billy.'

'Yes.'

'Well, shit, we just gotta 'ave a party.' Carlton half-smiles.

'We gotta get more drink, but,' he adds.

Carlton and Rennie drive off to town in Billy's car. When they leave, Billy feels unsure and alone. His mother just stares at him. Phyllis keeps her eyes glued on the mound of her womb and the grandparents crow to Darcy, camp talk he cannot understand.

The cousins burst through the door with a carton that Carlton drops on the table, then he turns to his brother. His smooth face holds the look of a small child who is about to show his father something he has achieved. His dark lips twitch as they try to keep from smiling.

' 'Appy birthday, Billy, ya ole cunt,' Carlton says, and produces a shining gold watch from the ragged pocket of his black jeans.

'It even works, Billy,' grins Rennie from beside his woman, so Darcy and China laugh.

The laughter swirls around the room like dead leaves from a tree.

They drink. They talk. Darcy goes home and the old people go to bed. His mother has not talked to Billy all night. In the morning he will buy her some pretty curtains for the windows and make a proper door and buy her the best dress in the shop.

They chew on the sweet cud of their past. The memories seep through Billy's skin so he isn't William Woodward the talented football player and artist, but Billy the wild, half-naked boy, with his shock of hair and carefree grin and a covey of girls fluttering around his honey body.

Here they are – all three together again, except now young Rennie is almost a father and Carlton has just come from three months' jail. And Billy? He is nowhere.

At last, Carlton yawns and stretches.

337 *glue sth. on sth. fix* sth. on sth.
337 *mound* thing that is large and round (e.g. a small hill)
338 *crow* (sl) talk in a way that is difficult to understand
345 *ole cunt* (sl) (here) term of friendship
357 *cud* food which has already been chewed
360 *covey* bunch, group

'I reckon I'll 'it that bed.' Punches his strong brother gently on the shoulder. 'See ya t'morrow, Billy, ole kid.' He smiles.

Billy camps beside the dying fire. He rolls himself into a bundle of ragged blankets on the floor and stares into the fire. In his mind he can hear his father droning away, telling legends that he half-remembered, and his mother softly singing hymns. Voices and memories and woodsmoke drift around him. He sleeps.

He wakes to the sound of magpies carolling in the still trees. Rolls up off the floor and rubs the sleep from his eyes. Gets up and stacks the blankets in a corner, then creeps out to the door.

Carlton's eyes peep out from the blankets on his bed.

'Where ya goin'?' he whispers.

'Just for a walk.'

'Catch ya up, Billy,' he smiles sleepily. With his head-band off, his long hair falls every way.

Billy gives a salutation and ducks outside.

A watery sun struggles up over the hills and reflects in the orange puddles that dot the camp. Broken glass winks white, like the bones of dead animals. Several children play with a drum, rolling it at each other and trying to balance on it. Several young men stand around looking at Billy's car.

He nods at them and they nod back. Billy stumbles over to the ablution block: three bent and rusty showers and a toilet each for men and women. Names and slogans are scribbled on every available space. After washing away the staleness of the beer he heads for the waterhole, where memories of his father linger. He wants – a lot – to remember his father.

He squats there, watching the ripples the light rain makes on the serene green surface. The bird calls from the jumble of green-brown-black bush are sharp and clear, like the echoes of spirits calling to him.

He gets up and wanders back to the humpy. Smoke from fires wisps up into the grey sky.

Just as he slouches to the edge of the clearing, a police van noses its way through the mud and water and rubbish. A pale, hard, supercilious face peers out at him. The van stops.

'Hey, you! Come here!'

The people at the fires watch, from the corner of their eyes, as he idles over.

'That your car?'

Billy nods, staring at the heavy, blue-clothed sergeant. The driver growls, 'What's your name, and where'd you get the car?'

366 *'it that bed = hit that bed* (infml) go to sleep
371 *drone* talk in a low monotone tone
375 *carol* sing in a group
391 *ablution block* (here) washing and toilet facilities
397 *squat* hocken, kauern
399 *jumble* disorderly group of things
402 *wisp* move in a long thin line
403 *slouch* walk in a slow tired way
405 *supercilious* arrogant
408 *idle* ['aɪdl] walk in a slow way

'I just told you it's my car. My name's William Jacob Woodward, if it's any business of yours,' Billy flares.

The sergeant's door opens with an ominous crack as he slowly gets out. He glances down at black Billy, who suddenly feels small and naked.

'You any relation to Carlton?'

'If you want to know –'

'I want to know, you black prick. I want to know everything about you.'

'Yeah, like where you were last night when the store was broken into, as soon as you come home causing trouble in the pub,' the driver snarls.

'I wasn't causing trouble, and I wasn't in any robbery. I like the way you come straight down here when there's trouble –'

'If you weren't in the robbery, what's this watch?' the sergeant rumbles triumphantly, and he grabs hold of Billy's hand that has marked so many beautiful marks and painted so many beautiful pictures for the wadgula people. He twists it up behind Billy's back and slams him against the black blue side of the van. The golden watch dangles between the pink fingers, mocking the stunned man.

'Listen. I was here. You can ask my grandparents or Darcy Goodrich, even,' he moans. But inside he knows it is no good.

'Don't give me that, Woodward. You bastards stick together like flies on a dunny wall,' the driver sneers.

Nothing matters any more. Not the trees, flinging their scraggly arms wide in freedom. Not the people around their warm fires. Not the drizzle that drips down the back of his shirt onto his skin. Just this thickset, glowering man and the sleek oiled machine with POLICE stencilled on the sides neatly and indestructibly.

'You mongrel black bastard, I'm going to make you – and your fucking brother – jump. You could have killed old Peters last night,' the huge man hisses dangerously. Then the driver is beside him, glaring from behind his sunglasses.

'You Woodwards are all the same, thieving boongs. If you think you're such a fighter, beating up old men, you can have a go at the sarge here when we get back to the station.'

'Let's get the other one now, Morgan. Mrs Riley said there were two of them.'

He is shoved into the back, with a few jabs to hurry him on his way. Hunches miserably in the jolting iron belly as the van revs over to the humpy. Catches a glimpse of his new Kingswood standing in the filth. Darcy, a frightened Rennie

415 *ominous* threatening
424 *snarl* speak in a deep nasty way
434 *mock sb.* make fun of sb. in a nasty way
439 *dunny* (AustEng) outdoor toilet
442 *drizzle* light rain
443 *thickset* stämmig
444 *sleek* elegant and simple
444 *stencil sth.* write sth. with a stencil (= Schablone)
446 *mongrel* (derog) person of mixed descent
450 *boong* (AustEng derog sl) Aborigine
452 *sarge* (infml) sergeant
455 *jab* blow
456 *jolt* shake, move up and down
457 *rev* (infml) drive with a loud noise (as the engine is in a low gear)

and several others lean against it, watching with lifeless eyes. Billy returns their gaze with the look of a cornered dingo who does not understand how he was trapped yet who knows he is about to die. Catches a glimpse of his brother being pulled from the humpy, sad yet sullen, eyes downcast staring into the mud of his life – mud that no one can ever escape.

He is thrown into the back of the van.

The van starts up with a satisfied roar.

Carlton gives Billy a tired look as though he isn't there, then gives his strange, faint smile.

'Welcome 'ome, brother,' he mutters.

460 *dingo* wild Australian dog

Tasks

1 Explain what the term 'home' means to you.

2 Outline Billy Woodward's biography using the information from the short story.

3 Examine Billy's attitude towards:
a) Aboriginal people;
b) white people.

4 Comment on the behaviour of the white barman and the policeman towards Billy.

5 HW Assess what Billy's identity is in Australian society. Take into consideration the world in which he lives, the world from which he comes, the reaction of people to him and the title of the short story.

6 Compare Billy's problem with identity with the problems of the half-castes in 'Marlene' (p. 30).

7 With a partner write one of the two following dialogues:
a) After his arrest Billy has to stand trial for theft. Write the dialogue between Billy and the prosecuting lawyer at the court hearing.
b) Write a dialogue between Carlton and Rennie which expresses their attitude towards Billy.

8 Describe the atmosphere at the beginning of the text and analyse the techniques and devices the author uses to create it.

Additional Text:
Will Storr The Dark Heart of Australia

When an Aboriginal man was killed by five white youths in Alice Springs in 2009, it was the latest race-hate crime in an area plagued by violence. What angered many Aborigines was the judgement given by the court.

The phone call came on 26 July last year. It was Kwementyaye's elder brother Darryl. He was sobbing. 'Where are you? You don't know, do you? Get round here now. It's my bros. They've found him at the bottom of Anzac Hill. He's dead.'

The first feeling was no feeling at all. Jade simply put the phone down. She'd met Kwementyaye two and a half years earlier, in Bojangles bar in Alice Springs. She was a relative newcomer to Alice. She was 28 and had travelled all over Australia, but she liked it here and she definitely liked the look of the handsome Alice-born native in the flashy cowboy hat. Protected from shyness by an armour of beer, she walked up and pinched his bum. They got together immediately. They made plans. They would work, save and marry. They would travel to southeast Asia.

How can all of that disappear in the space of a phone call? For Jade, it was simply too much to grasp.

The last time Therese Ryder saw her son Kwementyaye, he was dancing to country music. He'd just returned from Trephina Gorge, where he worked as a trainee ranger and was singing and clapping to his favourite tunes before a beery night out. The next morning, an old school friend of Kwementyaye's knocked on the door. Therese laughed when she saw him – he was dressed as a policeman.

'Why are you dressed like that?' she said.

'I'm a police officer now, Mrs Ryder.'

When he told her why he'd come, she screamed.

It was the sight of Therese and her family, sitting on the floor wailing and crying, that finally triggered Jade's tears. But there was mystery, too. How did Kwementyaye come to have abrasions and swelling on his face, arms, forehead and leg and a 3cm laceration on the back of his head? He wasn't the violent kind. He'd never been in trouble with the police. Perhaps, they thought, he'd been in a car crash. Soon, the police came with darker news: they believed Kwementyaye had been murdered.

In the streets and pubs and dusty camps of Alice Springs there were whispers and dread and fury; some heard rumours of white men fleeing the scene; others warned of riot and revenge. Bloody memories began to rouse themselves from the floor of the town's

3 *bros* (sl) brother
4 *Anzac Hill* name of a hill in the middle of Alice Springs
18 *ranger* person who protects and preserves parklands
19 *beery* (infml) involving drinking a lot of beer
27 *wail* make a long loud cry
28 *abrasion* Abschürfung
29 *laceration* deep cut in a person's flesh or skin
37 *rouse yourself* lift yourself

collective conscious. Worried, the police announced that race was not a motive in the crime. When reporters asked how they could know this when they didn't have any suspects, they replied: 'That's just what we're saying.'

[...] Before long, local men Scott Doody, Timothy Hird, Anton Kloeden, Joshua Spears and Glen Swain, all in their late teens or early 20s, were charged with murder and eight counts of recklessly endangering life.

The news crackled through the streets of Alice. Black worried to black and white worried to white. Nobody knew what would happen next. There were short-lived rumours that a memorial to Kwementyaye had been deliberately burned. Kwementyaye's mother feared a riot and the family issued a public appeal for calm. Two hundred and fifty locals paid for a full-page advert in the *Centralian Advocate* calling for peace. [...]

During my time in Alice Springs I quickly realised that before I could truly understand the events surrounding the killing of Kwementyaye Ryder, I'd first have to learn something of the history of the town itself. Marooned in the centre of an impossible universe of sand and heat, it has the air of an abandoned space station – alien and stagnant; desperate and defiant. If it feels lost in space, it also feels lost in time.

The story behind the friction [between whites and Aborgines] begins in 1860, the year the first white man passed through the district. By 1881 the whole of Central Australia was held by pastoralists or under lease application. Of course, the Arrernte people already lived here, and had done so for more than 50,000 years. They mounted a brief insurgency and suffered disease, gunfire and rape. The last major atrocity was triggered by a fight about an indigenous woman that lead to a white dingo trapper being murdered. The Europeans' revenge was 1928's Coniston massacre, during which it is thought that around 100 men, women and children were slaughtered.

Having been forced off their land, and with nowhere to find food and water, the Arrernte gathered in camps around the nascent town. There were regular attempts to eradicate these settlements. They were frequently raided, their inhabitants denied basic services, such as water. Between 1928 and 1964 there were at least four round-ups and forced evacuations and indigenous people were banned from entering Alice Springs. Today, Aboriginals from remote communities are still drawn here, to visit family, collect welfare or seek medical attention. Many sleep, as they did then, on the Todd. The camps remain, as does much of the dangerous energy. Eighty-two per cent of the local prison population is black. Alice Springs is reportedly the most heavily

56 *marooned* (here) in a remote place
58 *stagnant* motionless
58 *defiant* [dəˈfaɪənt] hostile
62 *pastoralist* (AustrEng) sheep or cattle farmer
63 *lease application* Antrag auf Pacht oder Miete
65 *insurgency* [ɪnˈsɜːdʒənsi] revolt
66 *atrocity* extremely cruel act, usu. involving murder
68 *Coniston massacre* massacre of Aboriginal Australians in revenge for the supposed murder of a white hunter
72 *nascent* [ˈneɪsənt] not yet fully developed
80 *on the Todd* along the Todd river

policed town in Australia – while the national average is one police officer per 375 citizens, Alice Springs's ratio is 1:135. [...]

That afternoon I hear a view of the recent troubles from local Greek-Australian art dealer Marilena Hippis. 'It's always been a very racist place, but tensions are rising,' she tells me. 'What's frustrating for white people is that we've got to fight for everything and they get $35 a week and here's a grant and here's a place in uni – just wake up in the morning and go to work. And they won't. You know what I mean? It shits me that they spit in the street. It shits me that they piss in the street. It shits me that they go to the pub in a filthy state.' She adds that she's finding herself increasingly intimidated by drunk indigenous people. 'I used to walk down the Mall and the Todd River at night, but there's no way I'd do it now. Things just seem a little more sinister, more dangerous.'

Marilena's attitude is fascinating because she's not someone who can be easily accused of racism – her husband is Aboriginal. [...]

The trial of the 'Ute Five' began in the middle of December 2009. The *Centralian Advocate* was there and reported with titillating colour: 'Defence lawyers had quiet words with the parents of the men, while a row of pretty young things, with painted nails and highlights in their hair, shared nervous giggles as they waited for the court to open... Mr Ryder's family slipped in the back. Scrutinising their every move was a line of journalists – some from out of town.'

With each eyewitness that testified, another mystery retreated and the truth, in all its halting savagery, began to assemble itself in the minds of Kwementyaye's family.

When they motored to the Todd river, all of the defendants except driver Kloeden were drunk. Despite the recent troubles in town and the men's subsequent actions, the defence claimed their intention was not to harass Aboriginals, but to check if it was possible to drive to the old Telegraph Station, 6 km upriver. Kwementyaye – who'd returned home from a night out only to discover that he had run out of cigarettes – visited the Todd to see if he could blag one from the campers. Falling into conversation with a group, he decided to stay.

The first time Kloeden drove at the campers he missed Tony Cotchilli's blanket by around a metre. Reaching the Telegraph Station, and finding himself unable to exit the river, he turned back. The second time he drove at the campers, he ran straight over Cotchilli's blanket, the old man scrabbling to hide behind a tree. Two campers testified that the men were swearing at them, shouting 'niggers' and 'black bastards' and that they 'stink'. In

89 *grant* sum of money given by the government for a particular purpose
94 *intimidate sb.* frighten or threaten sb
102 *titillating* exciting
107 *scrutinise sb./sth.* watch sb./sth. carefully
109 *testify* say in a court of law what you saw
110 *savagery* primitive violence
115 *harass sb.* jdn belästigen, jdn. schikanieren
119 *blag sth.* (sl) obtain sth.

retaliation, one woman threw a burning log at the disappearing 4WD. Kloeden drove on for a few hundred metres and stopped. The men shouted more racist abuse. Then they drove home to fetch a gun – a replica of a Colt 45 – and some blank ammunition and returned. En route, Hird fired out of his window. The car stopped so he could unjam the gun. Job done, he pointed it at the campers and fired again.

Terrified, the Aboriginal people scattered. Driving on, the 4WD passed Kwementyaye. Enraged, he threw a bottle at the vehicle. It hit. Kloeden braked. He did a U-turn and drove directly at him, stopping just in time, with Kwementyaye grabbing the bull-bars. Realising he was in serious trouble, he ran.

All four passengers jumped out of the car and chased Kwementyaye, who fell at the spot where his memorial can now be found. Hird ran up and kicked him in the head. Swain joined in, kicking him twice more in the head. Spears hit him over the back of the head with a bottle. 'Don't fuck with us,' one of them shouted. Then, car headlights startled them. They noticed Kwementyaye wasn't moving. 'Let's go! Let's go! Let's go!' shouted Swain. They fled and concocted an alibi in an attempt to fool the police.

The pathologist who examined Kwementyaye's body said he'd died from a haemorrhage at the base of the brain. While he had no evidence of a pre-existing aneurysm that was sensitive to rupture, he considered it likely that Kwementyaye had one because the physical damage to his body didn't appear acute enough to cause death.

The defence seized on this, positing that this theoretical aneurysm could have ruptured when Kwementyaye fell, rather than when he was beaten about the head. Despite this, the evidence seemed clear and devastating. Things, for the five young men, looked grim.

Throughout the trial, Kwementyaye's mother, Therese, couldn't draw enough strength to sit in court. 'I couldn't face those fellas,' she says. 'But I went on the day of sentencing. They walked in all dressed up neatly, the star attraction of the court. I burst out crying. I had to get out. I sang out to them, "You all look good on the outside, but inside there's bloody racism, straight out."'

It became obvious that something extraordinary was going to happen when Chief Justice Brian Martin began his pre-sentencing remarks. Strewn among the clauses are the stentorian admonishments you'd expect – words like 'drunk', 'stupid', 'violent' and 'aggressive' – but in almost every moment that matters, Martin excuses the 'relatively minor violence' he found took place.

128 *retaliation* attack in return for a similar attack
133 *unjam sth.* unblock sth.
147 *concoct sth.* invent sth.
150 *aneurysm* ['ænju:rɪsm] excessive swelling of an artery
150 *rupture* break open suddenly
154 *posit sth.* put forward sth. as an idea to be considered seriously
161 *fella* (infml) fellow, person
167 *Chief Justice* chief judge in Northern Territory
168 *stentorian* loud and powerful
168 *admonishment* warning

He accepted that their motive for driving up and down the Todd was not to harass black people. Of Kloeden's terrorising of campers, he said, 'As your counsel put it, you were hooning. Another word is lairising' and that he 'aimed to miss'. He absolved everyone but the driver for this, saying, 'Mr Kloeden, I pause in this sequence to observe there is nothing in the material before me to suggest that anyone in the car suggested that you drive at or close to the camp. This was your decision alone.' He accepted the defence's claim that there was 'no sinister purpose' in their driving home to fetch the pistol: 'You only wanted to have fun by firing it and making a loud noise as you drove around.' The racist abuse they shouted was downgraded to mere 'abuse'. He accepted the defence's bold claim that all of Ryder's physical injuries could have been caused when he fell. Although he initially acknowledges that 'it's not known precisely what caused the bleeding' that killed Ryder, in the crucial 'sentencing factors' section, he becomes absolute, saying: 'The deceased was susceptible to dire consequences from minor trauma by reason of a pre-existing aneurysm. But for the bursting of the aneurysm, the deceased would have suffered relatively minor injuries and the offenders would have been guilty of an assault at the lower scale of seriousness for offences of assault.' He said: 'None of you intended to cause serious harm'; that 'each of you has always got on well with Aboriginal people. However, on this occasion your normal attitudes and standards of behaviour were pushed to the background.'

Before the trial, an editorial in the *Centralian Advocate* acknowledged the importance of what was about to happen: 'Everyone knows this is a test case of Australian justice; a case where justice must be seen to be done. And in the Northern Territory a life sentence means life.' And life was exactly what Therese Ryder wanted: 'I know blackfellas who have got 10 years for domestic abuse. I wanted them in prison for a long time.'

Because Justice Martin decided that none of Kloeden's passengers had encouraged him to drive at the Aboriginals, he alone was found guilty of recklessly endangering life. Having already had their charge reduced from murder to manslaughter by recklessness, Martin found the five guilty of the even lesser crime of manslaughter 'by negligence'. Announcing a further 'reduction of your sentence by reason of your guilty plea and genuine remorse', he gave them between 12 months and six years. With parole, they'll be out in no more than four. [...]

According to Therese, it's only lucky that the Ryders are peaceful, practising Catholics: 'If this happened to [notoriously fierce] Warlpiri people, they'd have been coming in in busloads, with

175 *hoon* (AustrEng) behave like a hooligan
176 *lairising* (AustrEng) showing off
189 *the deceased* [di'si:st] (fml) the dead person
190 *dire* serious, urgent
209 *manslaughter* Totschlag
211 *negligence* ['neglɪdʒəns] failure to take proper care of sth.
212 *plea* Bekenntnis
212 *remorse* deep regret

spears and boomerangs. They'd have rushed into the courtroom and started fighting people.'

Today, Therese finds it very hard to sleep. She gets up in the early hours and cries. 'I pray to Jesus to look after me, but I can see no future. There are no happy times any more.'

And there's since been a further calamity. Devastated over the death of his 'bros', Darryl Ryder has disappeared. 'The last time we heard from him was October,' says Therese. 'I think, 'Don't say I've lost another son now.' We've got blackfella culture. When things like this happen, they go for revenge.'

'Do you think, when they're released, the five will be at risk?' I ask.

She looks unblinkably at her hands and says very quietly: 'That's not up to me. It's up to other families.'

From: *'Australia's Dark Heart',* The Observer, *3 October 2010*

223 *calamity* catastrophe

Tasks

1 Recount the crime told in the story.

2 Explain why there is tension between the white Australians and Aborigine Australians. (53-84)

3 Comment on the judge's verdict.

4 Imagine Billy read this article and wrote a letter-to-the-editor about his reaction. Write the letter.

TIM WINTON **Neighbours**

Tim Winton was born in 1960 in Perth, Western Australia. He has written many novels and collections of short stories. His epic novel *Cloudstreet* (1992) was adapted for the theatre. Two of his novels, *The Riders* (1995) and *Dirt Music* (2002) were shortlisted for the Booker Prize. Winton has won critical acclaim for his vivid descriptions of people and places in his stories. His recurring themes are the question of good and evil and the search for meaning.

Australia is an immigrant country. Tim Winton's short story 'Neighbours' (1985) gives an example of the rich diversity of cultural life in the suburbs of Australian cities and how it can affect those who come from a more traditional Australian background.

When they first moved in, the young couple were wary of the neighbourhood. The street was full of European migrants. It made the newly-weds feel like sojourners in a foreign land. Next door on the left lived a Macedonian family. On the right, a widower from Poland.

The newly-weds' house was small, but its high ceilings and paned windows gave it the feel of an elegant cottage. From his study window, the young man could see out over the rooftops and used-car yards the Moreton Bay figs in the park where they walked their dog. The neighbours seemed cautious about the dog, a docile, moulting collie.

The young man and woman had lived all their lives in the expansive outer suburbs where good neighbours were seldom seen and never heard. The sounds of spitting and washing and daybreak watering came as a shock. The Macedonian family shouted, ranted, screamed. It took six months for the newcomers to comprehend the fact that their neighbours were not murdering each other, merely talking. The old Polish man spent most of his day hammering nails into wood only to pull them out again. His yard was stacked with salvaged lumber. He added to it, but he did not build with it.

Relations were uncomfortable for many months. The Macedonians raised eyebrows at the late hour at which the newcomers rose in the mornings. The young man sensed their disapproval at his staying home to write his thesis while his wife worked. He watched in disgust as the little boy next door urinated in the street. He once saw him spraying the cat from the back step. The child's head was shaved regularly, he assumed, in order to make his hair grow thick. The little boy

1 *wary* cautious, mistrustful
3 *newly-weds* couple that just got married
3 *sojourner* person who stays in one place only for a limited amount of time
7 *paned* having lots of small window panes (= Scheiben)
9 *Moreton Bay fig* type of Australian fig tree
11 *docile* ['deʊsaɪl] easy to handle, peaceful
11 *moulting* ['məʊltɪŋ] losing hair
15 *daybreak watering* (here) act of urinating after getting up
16 *rant* speak or shout noisily and continually
20 *stack sth.* pile sth. up
21 *salvaged lumber* disused pieces of wood and furniture
25 *thesis* ['θi:sɪs] Doktorarbeit
27 *spray sth.* sprinkle sth. with liquid (here: urine)

stood at the fence with only his cobalt eyes showing; it made the young man nervous.

In the autumn, the young couple cleared rubbish from their back yard and turned and manured the soil under the open and measured gaze of the neighbours. They planted leeks, onions, cabbage, brussels sprouts and broad beans and this caused the neighbours to come to the fence and offer advice about spacing, hilling, mulching. The young man resented the interference, but he took careful note of what was said. His wife was bold enough to run a hand over the child's stubble and the big woman with black eyes and butcher's arms gave her a bagful of garlic cloves to plant.

Not long after, the young man and woman built a hen-house. The neighbours watched it fall down. The Polish widower slid through the fence uninvited and rebuilt it for them. They could not understand a word he said.

As autumn merged into winter and the vermilion sunsets were followed by sudden, dark dusks touched with the smell of woodsmoke and the sound of roosters crowing day's end, the young couple found themselves smiling back at the neighbours. They offered heads of cabbage and took gifts of grappa and firewood. The young man worked steadily at his thesis on the development of the twentieth century novel. He cooked dinners for his wife and listened to her stories of eccentric patients and hospital incompetence. In the street they no longer walked with their eyes lowered. They felt superior and proud when their parents came to visit and to cast shocked glances across the fence.

In the winter they kept ducks, big, silent muscovies that stood about in the rain growing fat. In the spring the Macedonian family showed them how to slaughter and to pluck and to dress. They all sat around on blocks and upturned buckets and told barely-understood stories – the men butchering, the women plucking, as was demanded. In the haze of down and steam and fractured dialogue, the young man and woman felt intoxicated. The cat toyed with severed heads. The child pulled the cat's tail. The newcomers found themselves shouting.

But they had not planned on a pregnancy. It stunned them to be made parents so early. Their friends did not have children until several years after being married – if at all. The young woman arranged for maternity leave. The young man ploughed on with his thesis on the twentieth century novel.

The Polish widower began to build. In the late spring dawns, he sank posts and poured cement and began to use his wood. The young couple turned in their bed, cursing him behind his back. The young husband, at times, suspected

33 *manure sth.* fertilize sth. by putting animal or plant waste on it
34 *measured* careful and controlled
34 *gaze* intense look
35 *leek* Lauch
35 *brussels sprout* Rosenkohl
35 *broad bean* Saubohne
37 *space sth.* place sth. at certain intervals
37 *hill sth.* form sth. (esp. soil) into a small mound
37 *mulch sth.* cover and protect sth. (esp. soil around a plant) with a mixture of dead leaves, straw, etc.
38 *resent sth.* feel angry and bitter about sth.
40 *stubble* short and stiff hair growing on a person's face or head
41 *garlic clove* Knoblauchzehe
46 *merge into sth.* mix with sth.
46 *vermilion* Zinnoberrot
48 *rooster* cock
58 *muscovy* type of large duck
60 *pluck* pull off the feathers
61 *dress* prepare for cooking
63 *haze* air which is difficult to see through
64 *down* Daunen
64 *fractured* broken
65 *intoxicated* excited and happy as if drunk
65 *sever sth.* cut sth. off
68 *pregnancy* Schwangerschaft
71 *maternity leave* Mutterschaftsurlaub
72 *plough on with sth.* keep on working hard at sth.
74 *sink a post* put a post in cement in the ground

that the widower was deliberately antagonising them. The young wife threw up in the mornings. Hay fever began to wear him down.

Before long the young couple realised that the whole neighbourhood knew of the pregnancy. People smiled tirelessly at them. The man in the deli gave her small presents of chocolates and him packets of cigarettes that he stored at home, not being a smoker. In the summer, Italian women began to offer names. Greek women stopped the young woman in the street, pulled her skirt up and felt her belly, telling her it was bound to be a boy. By late summer the woman next door had knitted the baby a suit, complete with booties and beanie. The young woman felt flattered, claustrophobic, grateful, peeved.

By late summer, the Polish widower next door had almost finished his two-car garage. The young man could not believe that a man without a car would do such a thing, and one evening as he was considering making a complaint about the noise, the Polish man came over with barrowfuls of woodscraps for their fire.

77 *antagonise sb.* make sb. angry on purpose
78 *throw up* sich erbrechen
78 *hay fever* Heuschnupfen
82 *deli* (infml) = *delicatessen shop* shop that sells food from other countries
87 *be bound to be* be certain to be
89 *booty* small woollen baby sock
89 *beanie* small hat worn by babies
89 *flatter sb.* say nice things about sb.
89 *claustrophobic* fearful of being confined or locked up
90 *peeved* annoyed, irritated
95 *barrowfuls of sth.* (here) plenty of sth.
96 *woodscraps* left-over pieces of wood

Infobox | Immigration to Australia

The official policy of all governments in Australia up to the 1950s was to exclude non-European people from immigrating to Australia. After World War II, Australia launched a massive immigration program, inviting displaced Europeans to the country. More than two million people immigrated to Australia from Europe during the 20 years following the end of the war. Although the British Isles remained the predominant source of immigrants, other European countries such as Greece, Italy, Germany, Yugoslavia became major contributors. This wave of immigration greatly changed the character of Australian society, which before the war had been largely British. The newcomers mostly lived in separate districts and kept their cultures alive. During the 1970s around 90,000 refugees from South-East Asia were resettled in Australia, making Australia a truly multicultural society. Nowadays about half of all immigrants come from East Asia and the Middle East. Today about 6% of the population is Asian. The change towards a multicultural society has not been without problems. There have been race riots in Australia, and a right-wing anti-immigrant party was successful in the late 1990s in Queensland. Immigration remains a sensitive topic in Australia.

Greek immigrants arrive in Sydney.

Labour came abruptly. The young man abandoned the twentieth century novel for the telephone. His wife began to black the stove. The midwife came and helped her finish the job while he ran about making statements that sounded like queries. His wife hoisted her belly about the house, supervising his movements. Going outside for more wood, he saw, in the last light of the day, the faces at each fence. He counted twelve faces. The Macedonian family waved and called out what sounded like their best wishes.

As the night deepened, the young woman dozed between contractions, sometimes walking, sometimes shouting. She had a hot bath and began to eat ice and demand liverwurst. Her belly rose, uterus flexing downward. Her sweat sparkled, the gossamer highlit by movement and firelight. The night grew older. The midwife crooned. The young man rubbed his wife's back, fed her ice and rubbed her lips with oil.

And then came the pushing. He caressed and stared and tried not to shout. The floor trembled as the young woman bore down in a squat. He felt the power of her, the sophistication of her. She strained. Her face mottled. She kept at it, push after push, assaulting some unseen barrier, until suddenly it was smashed and she was through. It took his wind away to see the look on the baby's face as it was suddenly passed up to the breast. It had one eye on him. It found the nipple. It trailed cord and vernix smears and its mother's own sweat. She gasped and covered the tiny buttocks with a hand. A boy, she said. For a second, the child had lost the nipple and began to cry. The young man heard shouting outside. He went to the back door. On the Macedonian side of the fence, a small queue of bleary faces looked up, cheering, and the young man began to weep. The twentieth century novel had not prepared him for this.

97 *labour* die Wehen
97 *abandon sth.* give sth. up
99 *black sth.* (here) polish sth.
99 *midwife* nurse who is trained to assist women in childbirth
101 *query* question
101 *hoist sth.* lift sth. up, raise sth.
107 *contractions* Wehen
110 *gossamer* (here) layer of sweat
110 *highlight sth.* emphasize sth., make sth. visible and prominent
111 *croon* speak in a low soft voice
114 *caress sb.* touch sb. with affection
116 *squat* Hocke
117 *sophistication* quality of being complex and having experience of life
117 *mottle* become covered with spots
118 *assault sth.* attack sth.
120 *wind* (here) breath
122 *trail sth.* draw sth. along behind
122 *cord* (hier) Nabelschnur
122 *vernix smears* greasy substance that covers the skin of a baby
127 *bleary* indistinct, not clearly visible

Tasks

1 Describe the young couple's new neighbourhood.

2 Examine the young couple's changing feelings towards the neighbours.

3 Evaluate the fundamental clash between the two groups, assessing what this also shows about Australian culture.

4 Analyse the point of view and its function.

5 Explain what the story implies about Tim Winton's attitude towards a multicultural Australian society.

1) 2) characterisation
3) narrative techniques
4) style, tone, register

Additional Text: Multiculturalism Is for Everyone

As a multicultural society Australia has adapted to people from different cultures coming to the country with their own traditions and ways of thinking. This text was written by a young intern at Actnow, a website that encourages young people to get involved in social issues.

Where would you be without the local Chinese takeaway? Or your daily cappuccino? These are just a few food clichés that help to identify what multiculturalism means to Australia, but what's actually beyond butter chicken and pad Thai? [...]

Multiculturalism is a cultural and political policy established by the Australian government to show citizens how they should live together.

The term multiculturalism means 'numerous cultures'. It was put into place to promote a way of thinking that embraces and accepts Australians who have come from different countries or who identify with a culture that is different from Anglo-Australian culture. This includes respecting peoples' choices and practices regarding their religion and their social beliefs. It means that all cultures are respected and nobody is more important than anyone else.

Multiculturalism as a political policy also emphasises that while Australians accept and recognise cultural diversity, all citizens identify one 'common law' and democratic government as their own.

The multiculturalism policy can be seen through the following core principles:

- Equality – this means all citizens are given equal rights, no matter what race or religion they are. It also ensures that people can rely on Australian law if they are discriminated against because of their cultural beliefs.
- Responsibility – this means all Australians are responsible for accepting others who have individual beliefs. It also means that we have a duty to support our democratic model of government.
- Benefits – this means we recognise that multiculturalism brings great benefits to society. And, if we continue to live in a society like this, the possibilities of success in social and business spheres are endless.

[...] After World War II (1945 onwards) Australia started receiving a large number of immigrants from Europe and the Middle East, and later Asia. Until this time, Australia was mainly populated by Irish and English immigrants and their descendants. This meant

4 *butter chicken* Indian chicken recipe
4 *pad Thai* Thai national dish
18 *common* that is for everyone
21 *core* central or most important part

that during the 1950s there was large increase in people with other cultures and religions.

During the 1960s the Australian government started to realise that immigrants were being unfairly treated, despite upholding Australian laws and making significant contributions to society. Many migrants and their families, particularly those who did not speak English, were also struggling to gain access to services like education and health care. By 1968, it had become obvious that a new and different approach to immigrant services was needed.

In 1973 the term 'multiculturalism' was introduced by the Labor government under Prime Minister Gough Whitlam. This led to the formation of migrant associations and advisory boards that looked specifically at issues affecting cultures and languages other than English. [...]

Australia doesn't have a formal document for a national cultural policy concerning multiculturalism. Instead, the government has a general policy. It provides a broad framework of cultural objectives and can be continuously updated. [...]

The values of multiculturalism are taught to children in primary schools, and are emphasised throughout the public education system. A number of state and federal laws, including equal opportunity and anti-discrimination laws, are also influenced by the key principles of multiculturalism, such as equality.

Harmony Day is another example of how multiculturalism is recognised by Australians. It happens on the 21 March every year and celebrates the benefits of living in a multicultural country. Harmony Day coincides with the United Nations International Day for Elimination of Racial Discrimination. [...]

The multiculturalism policy affects everyone living in Australia. It is supported by our laws and influences many social and political agendas. It impacts on our everyday lives, more so than we probably think.

Multiculturalism has helped us understand other cultures. It contributes a lot to Australian society, but mostly it brings education, understanding and difference.

Multiculturalism brings heaps of other stuff too, like exotic foods and flavours from other countries! In Sydney, Leichhardt is known as our 'Little Italy' and in Haymarket you can find anything Chinese – from Chow Mien to Hong Kong fashion. In the inner-west suburb of Petersham you can find fantastic Portuguese Chicken and the list just goes on ...

Australian fashion, food and culture have all been affected by multiculturalism because it makes up what it means to be Australian.

43 *migrant* ['maɪgrənt] person who moves from one country to another
49 *advisory* having the role of giving professional advice
73 *heaps* (infml) lots

Tasks

1 Outline the Australian multiculturalism policy.

2 Name the underlying principles of this policy as well as its effects on Australian society.

3 Imagine the young man in 'Neighbours' read this article. Write a letter which he sends to the website, explaining his experience of multiculturalism.

4 One person made the following comment on this article: 'Multiculturalism is a good idea. The problem is that it does not really work on the ground. [...] In the end we keep talking on a very superficial level about money and food.'
What in your view makes for a successful multicultural society?

5 Search the internet for information on current race relations in Australia.

Acknowledgements

Short stories
p. 6 ff. 'How Muster-Master Stoneman Earned His Breakfast' by Price Warung (William Astley), first published in *The Bulletin* (1890). Reprinted in *Tales of the Convict System* (1892)
p. 18 ff. 'The Drover's Wife' by Henry Lawson, first printed in *The Bulletin* (1892). Reprinted in *While the Billy Boils*, Sydney: Angus & Robertson, 1896
p. 30 ff. 'Marlene' by Katherine Susannah Prichard, first published in *The Bulletin* (1938). Reprinted by permission of HarperCollins Publishers (Australia) / Curtis Brown (Australia)
p. 45 ff. 'Going Home' by Archie Weller, first printed in *Going Home*, Sydney: Allen & Unwin, 1986. © 1986 Archie Weller
p. 64 ff. 'Neighbours' by Tim Winton, first printed in *Scission and Other Stories*, Melbourne: Penguin Books, 1985. © 1985 Tim Winton. Reprinted by permission of David Higham Associates, London

Additional texts
p. 16 f. 'Egalitarianism in Australia' by Chad Swanson, from the website of Convict Creations: www.convictcreations.com/culture/egalitarianism.html
p. 27 'Now I'm Easy' by Eric Bogle, from the website of Eric Bogle: www.ericbogle.net
© Eric Bogle and Larrikin Music Pty Ltd.
p. 28 'Openness and Freedom' by D.H. Lawrence, from: *Kangaroo* by D.H. Lawrence, London: William Heinemann, 1923
p. 40 ff. 'The Sorry Speech' by Kevin Rudd, from: Kevin Rudd, 'Apology to Australia's indigenous peoples', 13 February 2008
p. 58 ff. 'The Dark Heart of Australia' by Will Storr, from 'Australia's Dark Heart', *The Observer*, 3 October 2010, www.guardian.co.uk/world/2010/oct/03/alice-spring-murder-racism.
© Guardian News & Media Ltd 2010
p. 68 f. 'Multiculturalism Is for Everyone', from 'Multiculturalism', the website of Actnow, 11 April 2006, www.actnow.com.au/Issues/Multiculturalism.aspx

Photos/Illustrations
Cover: Sydney Opera House: F1online / Topaz; traffic sign: F1online / Ruby
p. 6 John Oxley Library / State Library of Queensland; p. 8 ullstein bild / united archives; p. 11 ullstein bild / TopFoto; p. 14 ullstein bild / united archives; p. 18 Newspix / News Ltd / 3rd Party Managed Reproduction & Supply Rights; p. 20 Shutterstock / edella; p. 23 National Library of Australia / B. O. Holterman Archive; p. 30 State Library of New South Wales; p. 31 ullstein bild / heritage; p. 34 Corbis / Sygma / John Van Hasselt; p. 38 akg-images; p. 45 Newspix / News Ltd / 3rd Party Managed Reproduction & Supply Rights; p. 47 Bridgeman Berlin / Warnampi Tingari, 1980 (acrylic). Tjupurrula / Dick Pantimas (c. 1940–83) / Corbally Stourton Contemporary Art, Australia; p. 52 Picture Alliance / ZUMA Press; p. 64 ullstein bild / Friedrich; p. 66 Bridgeman Berlin / Migrants arriving in Sydney, 1966 (gelatin silver photo), Moore, David (1927–2003) / Art Gallery of NSW, Sydney, Australia / Gift of the Artist 1997; Map, p. 72 Dr. Volkhard Binder, Berlin

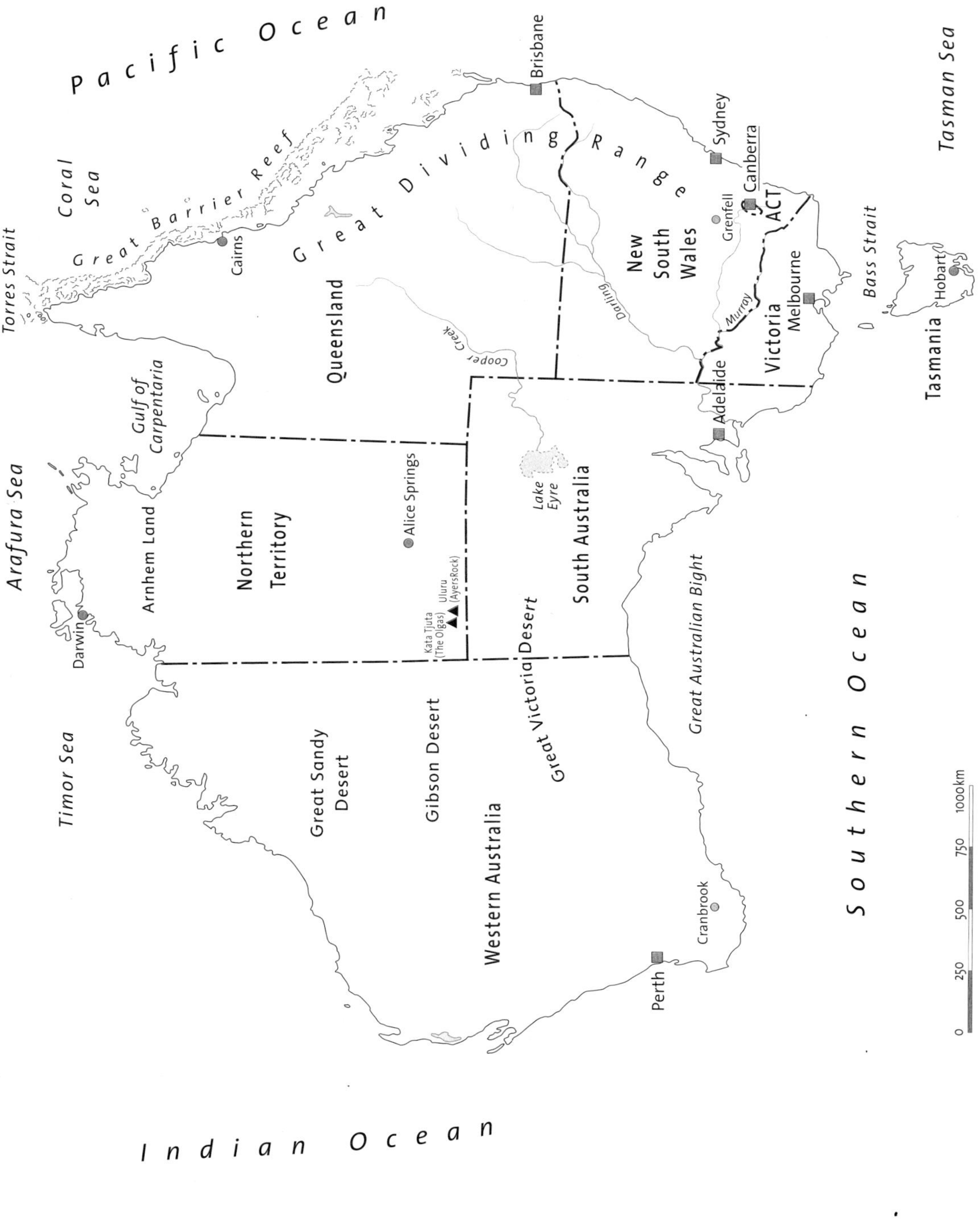
Pacific Ocean
Coral Sea
Torres Strait
Great Barrier Reef
Cairns
Great Dividing Range
Brisbane
Sydney
Canberra
ACT
Grenfell
New South Wales
Darling
Murray
Queensland
Cooper Creek
Gulf of Carpentaria
Arafura Sea
Arnhem Land
Darwin
Northern Territory
Alice Springs
Uluru (Ayers Rock)
Kata Tjuta (The Olgas)
Lake Eyre
South Australia
Adelaide
Victoria
Melbourne
Bass Strait
Tasmania
Hobart
Tasman Sea
Great Victoria Desert
Great Australian Bight
Southern Ocean
Timor Sea
Great Sandy Desert
Gibson Desert
Western Australia
Cranbrook
Perth
Indian Ocean
0
250
500
750
1000km